Mad Boy Chronicle

by Michael O'Brien

from

"GESTA DANORUM"
by Saxo Grammaticus   c. 1200 A.D.

and

"Hamlet, Prince of Denmark"
by William Shakespeare   c. 1600 A.D.

Playwrights Canada Press
Toronto • Canada

Mad Boy Chronicle © Copyright 1995 Michael O'Brien
Playwrights Canada Press is the publishing imprint of
the Playwrights Union of Canada (PUC): 54 Wolseley St., 2nd fl.
Toronto, Ontario CANADA M5T 1A5
Tel: (416) 703-0201 Fax: (416) 703-0059
e-mail: cdplays@interlog.com
Internet: www.puc.ca

Playwrights Canada Press operates with the generous assistance
of The Canada Council for the arts - Writing and Publishing Section,
and the Ontario Arts Council, Literature Office

Cover design by Tony Hamill.

Canadian Cataloguing in Publication Data
O'Brien, Michael 1965-
            Mad boy chronicle
A play
ISBN 0-88754-509-2
I. Title.
PS8579.B75M3   1996   C812'.54   C96-931228-8
PR9199.3.027M3   1996

First edition: July, 1996.
Second printing: November, 1997
Printed and bound by Hignell Printing, Winnipeg, Manitoba, Canada.

Mad Boy Chronicle

Michael O'Brien's previous plays include "The Last
Temptation of Christopher Robin" and "Freaks: A Circus
Tale With Music" at the National Arts Centre Atelier,
Ottawa. For Theatre Columbus in Toronto, he has created a
new musical, "The Barber of Seville", and for Young
People's Theatre he has created stage versions of "A
Christmas Carol" and "Oliver Twist". He lives in Toronto.

DEEPEST THANKS to all those
who lent the Mad Boy a hand:
Iris Turcott, Maja Ardal, Sally Han, Peter Hinton
Elliott Hayes, Kim McCaw, Banuta Rubess, Susan Serran
and a Legion of Fearless Actors.

THANKS TOO to Greg Spottiswood, Peter Smith, and
Janet Amos at the Blyth Festival for giving me a hideout.

UTMOST THANKS to:
Bob White, Michael Dobbin, Kathy Eberle
and the Crew who steered Mad Boy home.

THIS PLAY is dedicated to all those who dream
of slaughtering their Stepfathers.

- Michael O'Brien

Playwright's Foreword

I seem to remember starting this as a student in Montreal: sitting on the floor with a pile of mangled scripts. Among them was the infamous "Bad Quarto" of Shakespeare's "Hamlet"; another, *Gesta Danorum*, by Saxo Grammaticus, the Medieval source for the Hamlet story. With scissors and glue I put myself to work, trying to debase the greatest play of all time.

Soon, however, my sources weren't doing it for me. Eventually, I began tossing in a line or two of my own. Soon more lines appeared, the setting and scenes began to change, and so too did the names of all the characters.

After that, I stopped sitting on the floor. I threw away my sources, and the story began speaking in its own tongue. A brief hiatus followed, and the following summer, now a theatre school graduate, I slept in the back of a yellow van en route to the Edmonton Fringe. As far as I can remember, our driver hit a speed bump, a case of 24 beer fell on me, and lo! I had a title: "Mad Boy Chronicle".

For the next two years, I took shelter where I could find it, from the misty peaks of the Alberta Rockies to the snowbound Ontario houses infested with rats and ghosts. Along the way I scoped far and wide for inspiration — among my sources: "Hrafnkel's Saga" by some Icelandic monk, *The Rites of Man* by Rosalind Miles, *The Story of English* by Robert MacNeil and Co., and *Life Among the Wild Chimpanzees* by Jane Goodall.

Workshops, more workshops, more expanding, more surprises. If this was a "Hamlet" sendup, why were some parts making me cry? Meanwhile, my quest for Viking thrills continued to take me further and further afield — as I realized one afternoon in the Orkney Islands, fleeing the rush of the North Sea tide. Behind me was the tidal island home of someone named Thorfinn the Mighty. How exactly did I get there? I still cannot say.

I think at last it was in a hotel room in Calgary where the final dirty work got done. All those brutal questions like: What is this play about, really? And: How can we make this beast shorter?

About a third of the text was trimmed about this time.

Opening night I do not remember at all, except for Shaun Smyth at the cast party, standing on the bar and playing his bagpipes. And a lot of people howling at him, "Go, Mad Boy! Go, Mad Boy!" At last, I felt like a Sane Boy.

This is "Mad Boy Chronicle", my Viking Hamlet Saga. Only in Canada could such a play get writ. The question I get asked the most is: Should we take this play seriously, or is it just a big joke? The answer is, as always, yes.

— Michael O'Brien

"Mad Boy Chronicle" was workshopped at:

• Canadian Stage Company, Toronto, March, 1993, directed by Iris Turcott with Peter Hinton.

• The Banff Playwrights' Colony, summer, 1992 and 1994, directed by Kim McCaw.

•Theatre Passe Muraille, Toronto, August, 1994, directed by Banuta Rubess.

• final workshop and production - Alberta Theatre Projects, 1995.

"Mad Boy Chronicle" premiered at the Alberta Theatre Projects playRITES Fesitval, Calgary, Alberta, February, 1995 with the following cast:

INGA	*Donna Belleville*
ANNA/BROTHER PETRI	*Patricia Drake*
RAGNAR/GHOST	*Tom Rooney*
FENGO	*Hardee T. Lineham*
MATTHIUS	*Les Carlson*
LILJA	*Natascha Girgis*
GERUTHA	*Gale Garnett*
HORVENDAL	*Shaun Smyth*
BROTHER PAAVO	*Hugo Dann*
SONGMAN	*Kevin McGugan*
VIKINGS, MONKS ET AL	*Daryl Shuttleworth*
	Lenard Stanga
	Cory Mack
	Andrew Smith

Directed by Bob White.
Set design by John Dinning.
Costume design by Carolyn Smith.
Lighting by Brian Pincott.
Music by Kevin McGugan.
Production dramturg - Kathy Eberle.
Stage manager - Colin McCracken.
Assistant stage manager - Rose Brow.

CHARACTERS

FENGO, Lord of Helsingor.
GERUTHA, wife to Lord Fengo.
HORVENDAL, The Mad Boy.
MATTHIUS, friend to Lord Fengo
RAGNAR, son of Matthius.
LILJA, daughter of Matthius.

BROTHER PAAVO,
BROTHER PETRI, Christians.

INGA, an old woman.
ANNA, another old woman.

The GHOST of the dead chieftain, Horvendal the Elder.

Vikings, monks, wolves, spirits.

The Ghost Of Jesus Christ.

The Scene: Helsingor, Denmark.
999 A.D. Winter.

Running time: 2 hours, 16 minutes plus intermission.

Playwright's Note:

Spelling, punctuation and syntax are erratic to suggest emphasis, dialect, and state of mind.

This play was made possible by grants from The Canada Council and the Ontario Arts Council Playwright Recommender program.
— M. O'Brien

"Come on Mad Boy, you can do it!"

Shaun Smyth (l), Hardee T. Lineham (r) in the 1995 Alberta Theatre Projects production.

— photo by Trudie Lee Photography, Calgary.

Act One,
Scene One

Darkness. Night. The sound of a drum. The wind howls. Wolves howl. The smoke-filled hall at Helsingor, Denmark. Deep midwinter, 999 A.D. Viking dragonhead-posts stare northward.

Inside we hear a Viking winterfest. Singing, shouting, laughing, fighting, the smell of burning cedar in the air. Vikings rant and roar and drink and howl. One Viking sings lustily with a drum:

VIKING

Wealth must die, and Kindred die,
A Man himself must likewise die,
But Fame and Glory never die
For him who achieves it well.
Goats must die, and Kindred die,
A Man himself must likewise die,
But one thing is shall never die,
The Verdict on each Man who dies;
But one thing is shall never die,
The Verdict on each Man who dies...

Drums go quieter. Meanwhile, outside the village, INGA, an ancient fishwife, huddles in the snow. The black impenetrable forest looms beyond.

INGA

Listen to them. Listen to them festivitatin.
Howlin yowlin. Winterfest indeed.
Not a scrap nor spot o'human decencie,
Makin us poor old wimmen sit outside
I' the wind'n the ice'n the snow...

ANNA	Ahoy!
INGA	Who's that?
ANNA	Me!
INGA	Who's me?
ANNA	Your sister! Come from the feastin. Look what I filcht from the menfolk — look, dearheart, look!

She has a cooked rabbit and a jug of ale.

INGA	You didn't!
ANNA	Right off the fire.
INGA	I'm starv'd. Naeone saw ye?
ANNA	Too drunk they were.
INGA	Greedy dogs. Swine.
ANNA	I can't bide Lord Fengo. Can't bide his manner. Not that the last Lord were much better. Or the one afore that. Or his father afore him.
INGA	Aye, I'd like to flay the lot o'them, every last Viking.
ANNA	And roll'em in salt.
INGA	That'd teach'em.
ANNA	Oh well, one day everythin'll change and the world'll be wonderful.
INGA	Aye. And we'll be dead.
ANNA	Aye will we. May the stars protect us.

INGA   Now come on, give us some ale. Don't you be piggin it all, greedy.

> *They devour the rabbit. Wind howls in the distance. A drum beats.*
>
> *Behind them enters the GHOST of the late chieftain, Horvendal the Elder, in Viking burial dress. He brandishes a great war-axe and green smoke issues from his nose. Glowing embers hang from his hair and beard. He hisses. INGA turns.*

INGA   Hoy sister — look we gots company.

ANNA   Here piss off, we're trying to eat.

INGA   Go on then, have ye nothin else to do?
Be off with ye! Off I say!

ANNA   Ruffian! Hedge-hogg!

INGA   Arse-manglin curr!

ANNA   Aye, go cockwhallop someones else!

INGA   That's tellin him!

> *INGA throws a snowball. The GHOST vanishes. Pause.*

INGA   Hoy shite — wot was that?

ANNA   Wot?

INGA   Himm! That were himm!

ANNA   Who, sister?

INGA   Himm! The lord what's dead, sister, that were a blikkit ghost!

ANNA   Ohh the Lord o'the Slain protect us—

INGA   Horvendal the Elder. Oh twas a wicked mann. Chopt off me late husband's foot he did, just for the fun of aseein him hopp!

ANNA   I am agonna hide.

INGA   Me too.

Drums. The GHOST reappears.

ANNA   Naay he's back, he's gonna trundle us off to the spirit world! Inga, Inga throw a snowball at him!

INGA   You throw a bloody snowball at him!

ANNA   Here — we never hurt you! Haa! Go on wi'ye! Away you fierce and horrible tyrant! Back to yer grave!

She grabs a snowball.

GHOST   (*a ghostly whisper*) Hoorvendaaalll... Hoorvendaaall... Where - is - my - Sonn?

Pause.

ANNA   He ain't here.

GHOST   (*louder*) Hoorvendaaaaal...Hoorvendaaaaaal... Where - is - my - Sonn?

INGA   He ain't here, we say!

GHOST   (*roaring*) HOORVENDAAAAAL... HOORVENDAAAAAAL.... WHERE - IS - MY - SONN??

BOTH   Heeeellllppp!!

> *Thunder. ANNA screams. The GHOST vanishes.*
> *Blackout. Lights up. Pause.*

INGA   That spirit were ahowlin for his sonn.

ANNA   Wot?

INGA   That dead wretched spirit, sister, he were ahowlin for
                his sonn!

ANNA   I int gettin involvd!

INGA   No, don't you see? His soul, it's not yet at rest! It's
                up to us, to us, sister — to tells the Young
                Horvendal!

ANNA   You tell the boy. I int atellin him. He don't believe
                in spooks noways.

INGA   He will believe. He gotts to believe. I'll go find the
                boy, and make the boy believe!

> *INGA runs to the village. ANNA stays and*
> *drinks.*

ANNA   Oh Denn-Mark, Denn-Mark, ohh bastion of the
                brave,
                Folks int got the decencie to stay put i' their graves.

> *ANNA exits.*

***

Scenus Secundus

Meanwhile. The smoke-filled hall at Helsingor.

LORD FENGO sits surrounded by a mob of Vikings. He is very huge and very drunk, covered with food, and wears an eyepatch. He is having a laugh at the expense of LILJA, a thirteen-year-old girl. Further off sits GERUTHA, his wife.

FENGO   Bring the girl over here.

Vikings bring LILJA across the room.

Well, well prettygirl — how now, little thing? What say you to Fengo, Master o' the Northern Realm?

LILJA hides her face. The Vikings laugh.

I don't think yer daughter likes me, Matthius.

MATTHIUS   Course she do, Fengo, course she do. She's just in awe of ye, that's all.

FENGO   Have a drink with old Fengo, prettygirl.

MATTHIUS   Go on sweetheart, don't be afraid.

FENGO   Don't break me heart, sweet thing, come sit on my knee.

MATTHIUS   Aye!

LILJA   You are a fukkin animal, Fengo.

> *LILJA slaps him.*

MATTHIUS   Lilja!

FENGO   Haaaa! A child after me own heart! Come here! Smile at Lord Fengo, you rambunctious little filly!

MATTHIUS   I dunno where she gots her mouth from.

FENGO   Drink, bonnie lass. Drink Fengo's health! Heyup, hearties, hold the girl down. Your health, my little nordic beauty!

> *FENGO pours beer over her head. The Vikings laugh.*

LILJA   Help!

FENGO   What's the matter with the youth nowadays? They've all gone soft'n spoiled. Whats become of the Viking Spirit, Matthius? It wants reviving!

(*to LILJA*) Have ye ever seen Fengo's Hole? Fengo show yez Fengo's Hole. Nasty dirty eyesockett, nothin inside! Look, prettygirl, look!

> *FENGO pulls off his eyepatch and opens his eye socket. LILJA screams.*

Looks a bit like a rabbit's bum, don't it?

GERUTHA   Fengo stop—

FENGO   Why art afeard, girlie? It's a good honest Warr-Wound! Hoy Matthius — Matthius look! (*MATTHIUS cringes*) Haaa haaaa—

GERUTHA   Fengo, for the love of your fathers, stop!

FENGO   Ahhhh, I'm in a jolly mood.

LILJA runs out. FENGO finishes his ale.

| | I am Fengo: High Lord of Helsingor. Voted Lord Ruler by the Thunder-god hisself. It were Thorr what struck me dead brother down, seven years ago tonight. Stuck him down with a mighty meteor! Right Matthius? |

MATTHIUS   Aye, Fengo, aye!

FENGO   'Coward,' spake Thunder-god, unworthy to to be called Viking! Death to Dead Brotherlord. Long Live Lord Fengo!

MATTHIUS   Hail Hail!

VIKINGS   Long Live Lord Fengo!

FENGO   All hail Gerutha — Fengo's bride of seven years. Widowed wife of deadbrother lord; lawful holder of deadbrother's lands!

VIKINGS   Hurrah! Hail Gerutha!

FENGO   So woman, havin had both us bullies, which in yer mind were the better of us two? Was it Fengo? Hey? Was it merrie old Fengo? Was it dirty old Horvendal the Elder? Or was it Fengo? Hey? Hey missus? Hey, hey?

GERUTHA   It were you Fengo, it were you.

FENGO   Haaa! Did ye hear that? Hearties did ye hear the womann! Haaa! You saucy old thing! Give Fengo a kiss!

ALL   HURRAAAH!!

He kisses her obscenely. Pause.

FENGO	Somebody's missing. Somebody ain't here. Where's my adopted sonn? Where's my dear little boy?
GERUTHA	Asleep, Fengo. Don't wake him.
FENGO	Horvendal! Horvendal! I wants to talks to me sonn! HORVENDAL! Lord Fengo wants to speak to his ladd!

Lights up on young HORVENDAL, praying in the woodshed. He is 14 years old, short and scrawny, with crazed eyes.

HORVENDAL	Jesus, King of Heaven from the frozen edges of the earth, I beseech you—
FENGO	Hoy, ahoy, laddie!
HORVENDAL	Let not my heart be consumed by barbarous Hate—
FENGO	Show us yer face, shitthead!
HORVENDAL	From the sinns of Hate and Envy, from the sinns of Pride and Anger, from all thoughts of Evil gainst mine own flesh and blood deliver me Oh Christ Jesus, Redeemer of Men—

FENGO bursts in, followed by the rest.

FENGO	What's goin on in here?
HORVENDAL	God bless you, uncle.
FENGO	Don't you 'God bless me'. What're you hidin away for?
GERUTHA	He's makin silence, Fengo, amembrin of his Daa.
FENGO	Oohhhh faithful faithful boy. Amembrin of his Daa. His Daa what left him, his Daa he never knew! I'm yer Daa now sonn. You know that. Get up and gives yer Dadda a hugg.

HORVENDAL   Yer not my Paa.

FENGO   I is.

HORVENDAL   Yer NOT!

FENGO   I IS! Now what are you doin in here? Hey, laddie true? What're you doin in here then? Hey? Hey?

HORVENDAL   Praying.

FENGO   Praying?

HORVENDAL   Aye, to the Lord Christ the Merciful, the Son of Heaven and the God of Peace — who's gonna save Dennmark, Fengo — save it from the likes of you.

FENGO   Ho. Godd of Peace then, hey? Godd of Peace? See, Matthius? This is what I been talkin about. Yer a disgrace lad to yer own people, yer brave forefathers what fought'n died fer you. What is this new Godd, what wrenches sonns away from their fathers, tearin families and kingdoms apart — what in fucks wrong wi'ye anyways boy, are ye sick?

HORVENDAL   I forgives you, uncle.

FENGO   Forgives us — fer what?

HORVENDAL   For the violence you committed against God's Children, and the mockerie you hold against his name.

FENGO   Violence? Mockerie?

MATTHIUS   The boy talks gibberish! E'er since that Book turn'd up in yer plundersack he been a weird one, Fengo.

FENGO   Aye has he.

> *HORVENDAL has a bowl and towel. He kneels at FENGO's feet and washes them.*

HORVENDAL In the name of the Father, the Sonn and the Holy Spirit, I bow down, and pay you this respect.

FENGO What're you doing?

GERUTHA Horvendal...

FENGO Here — what're you washin my feet for?

HORVENDAL This is what the Lord Christ did.
He lov'd his enemies, like I love you.
God bless you, Uncle Fengo, dear Uncle Fengo
Peace.

> *Pause.*

FENGO Ha haaa! Lookit this! A Godd what washes people's feet! You see this bullies? Now Fengo's finally heard all.

> *They all laugh.*

Yer mother's been way too lenient. Way too soft on you, sonn. We'll have none of this love and peace prattle. Not while Fengo is Lord. Forgive me. He don't forgive me. He only forgives me cause he's afeard of me! Int that right, little laddie? Hey? Hey?

Go find yer Lord Jesus — tell him Fengo says he's a Womann! Tell him nobody never nail'd the Thunder-Godd to no Cross!

> *All laugh. FENGO rips up HORVENDAL's Bible.*

Still forgives us now, sonn? Go on, take a swing at me!

FENGO   Still forgives yer Uncle Fengo now? Hey? Hey?

                 Pause.

HORVENDAL   Yes, sir, I do.

FENGO   Liar!

                 FENGO spits on him.

GERUTHA   Fengo, please—

FENGO   Let's go Matthius, afore I cripple the boy.

                 *FENGO turns to leave. HORVENDAL prays
                 loudly.*

HORVENDAL   You what laughs — tomorrow shall you weep!
                 Doomed are the Mightie — they shall be laid low!
                 Scatter'd their swords shall be, hammer'd into
                 ploughshares!
                 And the Meek, the Weak, the Gentle and Oppress'd,
                 Shall rise, rise, to inherit the Earth!

                 Pause. FENGO turns again.

FENGO   What's that?

HORVENDAL   Thus spake the Christ.

FENGO   What's this says you, 'bout the Meek?

HORVENDAL   Praise the Power of the Lord.

                 Pause.

FENGO   Show us these Meek. Let me at them. We'll soon see
                 who inherits what. Meantime nephew, piddleprophet,
                 inherit this: I want you off my land by the crow o'the
                 cock, the morrow.

GERUTHA   Fengo, no—

FENGO   Stand up and fight me, sonn!

GERUTHA   Bless him, Fengo, he's a boy, he don't mean it!

FENGO   Ohhh yes he does.

HORVENDAL   Fengo, Christ he's acomin to Helsingor;
He'll be seekin for you Fengo, so he shall.

FENGO   Let him try it! I'll be ready. Let him stand, his Meek
against my Axe-menn. By the crow o the cock, let
your gutless face be gone. That's all lads. Fengo has
spoken.

MATTHIUS   Haill, Fengo!

VIKINGS   HAILL!!

FENGO   Move, woman.

MATTHIUS   Godd of Peace indeed.

> *MATTHIUS spits on HORVENDAL and exits
> with FENGO. GERUTHA is alone with
> HORVENDAL who gathers the pages of his
> Bible.*

GERUTHA   Horvendal, sweet Horvendal...

HORVENDAL   I nae wants to talk to you muther.

GERUTHA   Sonn, if din't marry him I'd be dead!

HORVENDAL   Death int such a bad thing.

GERTUTHA   Horvendal, sweet sonn, Jesus Christ is make-believe;
Howcome yer fakin, makin like he's real?

HORVENDAL	Jesus Christ is real Momma! All the world knows except for here! Jesus he's the Lord of Peace, he's awatchin oer us now! He's awatchin o'er the world, Momma! He can see inside yer heart!
GERUTHA	My heart — why do you wrench at it?
HORVENDAL	What you get is what you choose.
GERUTHA	Horvendal don't tear my love in half!
HORVENDAL	There's no love in you woman — only Fear.
GERUTHA	*Stop it!* Just stop it — undo this webb of ire! I'm sworn to you both! Cant you not clasp hands? Just ask his forgiveness — quit provokin his wrath. Fer the love of your warr-torn mother, Horvendal — please!
HORVENDAL	Hie off you Fengo-fucker. Go with your Mann.

Pause

GERUTHA	Yooou bastard — you blister — you vile, ungrateful hound! Fie upon you then — outt upon you — I have no sonn!

She spits at him and exits in tears,

HORVENDAL	The same to you!

Viking am I not, Viking I'll not be,
Too far and wide our bloody quest for Fame
Has devastated and disgraced the rolling earth!
And him — him — the worst and wickedest among us,
Still he stays our Chieftain — rooks me Maa!
Down down, you hateful rising furies,
Snarling massacre, back into my spleen!
I'm to Jerusalem, land of Peace and Freedom,
There will I meet Jesus, learn the ways of Peace!

HORVENDAL   (*continued*) Brave Horvendal, resists the urge to kill!
             Brave Horvendal, shall seek a better path!
             Brave Horvendal, whose name shall shine above all
             Saints!
             Whose name shall shine beside the name of Christ!
             Hallelujah!

             A knock on the door.

HORVENDAL   Who's there?

INGA   Young Horvendal?

HORVENDAL   Who is it?

INGA   A fishwife. Inga's my name.

HORVENDAL   What do you want?

INGA   Ooooh young Horvendal, I gots a terrible secret but
             I'm afeard to tell it ye.

HORVENDAL   Say it, and quickly!

INGA   There's a Ghost, lad, a Spirit i' the Forest,
             And he looks all the world like yer Daa.

HORVENDAL   What?

INGA   Green were his eyes, his face yellow,
             And he look'd all the world like yer Daa!

HORVENDAL   Get out!

INGA   Hooorvendaaal, he cried, Hooorvendaaal...
             Where - is - my - Sonn?
             Hooorvendaaal... Hooorvendaaal...
             Where - is - my - Sonn?

HORVENDAL   *Stop it*, you old biddy what believes in goblins and
            trolls. You're so full o fishtales there's nae room fer
            yer brains! Ghosts indeed. I had it wi' you people!
            Go tell it round the campfire you simple old crone.
            You blubbering old pagan be off with ye!

INGA   But sonn, sonn, yer Father he called fer ye! He wants
            to speak to ye. He do!

HORVENDAL   Away at once! I'll not hear another word! Protect me
            Jesus from these fools...

                Pause.

INGA   Think what you want, sonn. Do as you will,
            But choose the wrong path — it shall all come to ill.

                Pause. She exits. Pause.

HORVENDAL   What was this? Never mind. Come dawn,
            Horvendal from out this hell-hole shall be gone...

                            ***

Scenus Tertius

Before MATTHIUS' lodge. Morning. Enter
RAGNAR and MATTHIUS.

MATTHIUS   Liljaaa! Liljaaa! Where is that girl?

RAGNAR   She be starin out her window all sheepfaced again.
Put her to work, hey Father?

MATTHIUS   Aye I shall too. Gots to be good for somethin she.
Daughter!

RAGNAR   Me, I loves whale-huntin. I'll give the big fellow a
extra harpoon fer you.

MATTHIUS   That's me brave ladd. That's me stout and heartie
fella. But don't do nothin stupid will ye hey son? It
int wise.

RAGNAR   Nae fuss, Dadd.

MATTHIUS   Lilja! Lilja! Lilja, I say!

LILJA   (*off*) What?

MATTHIUS   Come say goodbye to yer brother. He's leavin.

LILJA   (*off*) Yeah, yeah.

MATTHIUS   Move it girl. And fast!

LILJA   (*off*) Yeah, yeah.

RAGNAR	You keep an eye on her, father. She's at that dangerous age.
MATTHIUS	Nae worry fer that, sonn. I'm trainin her good. Liljaaa!
LILJA	(*enters*) What?
RAGNAR	Lagabout girl.
MATTHIUS	Give yer brother a good luck charm as is the custom.
LILJA	Why?
RAGNAR	And hurry up too.
LILJA	I ain't got none.
RAGNAR	Cmon, anything'll do.
LILJA	Here brother, dear brother, ye want the scalp off me head? (*cutting her hair with a knife*)
RAGNAR	Girl!
MATTHIUS	What're ye doin?
RAGNAR	I can't be totin that at sea!
MATTHIUS	Give him yer stickpin instead, child, that's a nice gift.
LILJA	You gave it me, Paa!
MATTHIUS	Give it o'er or I'll smack ye.

She gives it to him.

LILJA	Here.
RAGNAR	Thank ye sister.

LILJA	Don't drown.
RAGNAR	And you obey yer father cause he knows what's what.
MATTHIUS	Aye it's true. I do.
LILJA	Can I go back to me bed now?
MATTHIUS	No, girl, he's not left!
RAGNAR	Here, she's mouthin off to you Daa — disrespectin her elders!
MATTHIUS	What? What's this?
LILJA	I'd never mouth off to you.
RAGNAR	Again again! She says it but she don't mean it. Watch her, she's double-tongued — a sheep and a serpent!
MATTHIUS	I'm tryin to be a good father to you, girl. We gotts to have order, that's all. Order! I wants the best, the best fer me girl — and fer me boy too.
RAGNAR	We gots the best father in all of Denn-Mark.
MATTHIUS	And I gotts the best kinn.
RAGNAR	We gotts the best Paa i' the World!
MATTHIUS	And I got — ohh, sonn!

> *They embrace. LILJA makes an obscene gesture*
> *at them both. RAGNAR sees her over*
> *MATTHIUS' shoulder. He seizes her by the hair*
> *and they fight.*

MATTHIUS	Here, children — what do I have to do fer you? Here, I loves you, I'd cut off both me arms! Think of yer Mother, had she aseen this scrappling — think of yer poor dead Mother! *Stop!* (*he pulls them apart*) We gotts to make us a solemn vow — to love and honour and protect one another. Sweet daughter, say yer sorry. Kiss yer brother. Now!

> *Pause.*

LILJA	Sorry, brother.
RAGNAR	Nae fuss, sister.
MATTHIUS	Go on —make the vow too.
RAGNAR	I won't let nobody hurts ye, sister.
LILJA	I won't let nobody hurts me neither.
MATTHIUS	Now cutt palms. Clasp hands. Make a ring. All three. Remember who we are. Who are we? We're DANES! The proudest, mightiest race on earth! And why? Why? The unbreakable Bond of Blood. Without that — without the Bond of Blood — The Lord o'the Gallows protect us — we're doomed!
RAGNAR	Aye doomed! Long Live Blood!
MATTHIUS	May the Great Odinn himself bless and protect this good family. The Great — and the Small. (*he pats LILJA's head*) Go, Brave Ragnar, out across the Sea — go kill a whalefish fer yer sister.

> *RAGNAR holds up his sword.*

RAGNAR	Aye, I shall, Father, I shall. In the name o' Skull-Byter, Sword o' me Granpapaa — I shall. Farewell, Father.

MATTHIUS   Farewell, sonn.

RAGNAR   Farewell, little sister.

LILJA   Aye.

RAGNAR   Ahoy — wait for me!

              *He runs off. LILJA turns to leave but
              MATTHIUS stops her.*

MATTHIUS   Sweet daughter, dear daughter, I know yer unhappy
              and fain would cheer ye.

LILJA   You need not father, I'm as happy as a barnacle.

MATTHIUS   I know it's hard to be the girl, my dear. I know it's
              hard, me lovin him more than you. But ye gots to
              accept yer lott in life. It's the godds' will.

LILJA   Aye, I do accept it. At least I'm not a horse.

MATTHIUS   That's the spirit. That's the familie spirit.
              Oh Lilja, Lilja, me sweet sweet pride and joy.
              A fine woman yer turnin out to be.

LILJA   You too, father.

MATTHIUS   Come, let's inside.

              She exits. He follows.

              ***

Scene The Fourth

Midnight. Miles away. The middle of a great frozen lake.

A full moon. Bitter cold. Wolves in the shadows. HORVENDAL trudges miserably through the snow.

HORVENDAL   Jerusalem! I can see it now;
Gilden it is, risin up to the sky!
Soon I'll be there, in front of Jesu's Fireplace,
Away from Helsingor. Away from Fengo!
There it is! Just the other side of that Forest.
Comin, Lord Christ — comin. I'm acomin.

He trudges on.

Jesus, this icy lake goes on and on!
How far away's this place asposd to be?
Weren't there a star or sommet hangin over Jerusalem?
All these friggin stars they look the same...
Christ? Lord Jesus? Is you a-heedin me?
If yer real, as yer Holybook sez,
Lift me up and fly me to yer Home!

Pause. A wolf howls.

Heyup Jesus, I done befaith'd in you!
Ye gotts to do me miracles — that's the deal!
Jesus? Jesus? Holy Lord Christ?
Yuz gots to gimme a guide or somethin, Jesus!
Helloooo? Hello? Lord Jesus?

Wolves howl louder. A raging voice in the wind.

GHOST   Hoorvendaaal...Hoorvendaaaal...
Where - is - my - Sonn?

HORVENDAL   Who's that? Father?

GHOST   HOORVENDAAAAL...HOORVENDAAAAL...
WHERE - IS - MY - SONNN??

A deep bang from below.

HORVENDAL   Jesus, there's somethin under the ice—

Bang. Bang.

A walrus perhaps, or one o'them killer whales—

Bang. Bang. Bang.

Mercy! Protect me! Angels and ministers of grace—

*He runs. The ice bursts open. The GHOST of the
dead lord rises up from the lake. He is twelve feet
tall, roaring and chanting, brandishing his sword,
surrounded by giant wolves.*

GHOST   HOOORVENDAL, BELOV'D OF THORR,
CHILD OF MURDER, CHILD OF WARR!
HEAR YE NOT THE SPIRITS' CRY?
LOOK INTO THY FATHER'S EYE!
HORVENDAL — LOOK UPON THY DESTINY!

HORVENDAL   Father? What happened to you?

GHOST   I *died*! I'm dead, sonn - that's whats happen'd to me!
I come from Valhalla, Afterlife of the Brave.
Listen, listen to my Tale, my Sonn:
Hoorvendaaaaal...Hoorvendaaaaaal...

HORVENDAL   You ain't real, Dadda—

GHOST   Thine Uncle—

HORVENDAL   I don't wanna hear this, Dadda—

GHOST   THINE UNCLE — IS A MURDERER!
Sweet Sonn, to tell the tale, unmanly Coward,
How he did stalk thy sleeping father in his sleep,
And crush his VIKING HEAD WITH A ANVILL—

HORVENDAL   It probably served you right, Dadda.

GHOST   AND HOW — HOW — that same unmanly Coward
Calls hisself a LORD!
And took his BROTHER'S WIFE!
Oh MOCKERY!
Oh HUMILIATION and DISGRACE!
Sonn of mine — art thou a Mann?

HORVENDAL   Please, Dadda—

GHOST   Sonn of mine — art thou a DANE?

HORVENDAL   Stop!

GHOST   Sonn of mine — art thou —
HORVENDAL THE YOUNGER?
And Most Fittest True High Lord of Helsingor?

HORVENDAL   NO! No, I renounce you father!
I don't wants to be no Lord of Helsingor!

>   *The GHOST lets out a howl and the earth
>   quakes.*

GHOST   You *seen* me bloody murder, sonn. Quit yer hidin.
Quit this childish sealin of yer soul.
You weren't yet seven. Hidden in a tree.
YOU SEEN ME DIE, sonn! Quit blockin it out!

HORVENDAL　You LIE!

GHOST　I raised you to be a Warrior —
A brave and mightie conqueror!
And now — now — your people need you most.
You turn and runn like a castout dogg?

HORVENDAL　Helllpp!

More thunder.

GHOST　HOORVENDAAL, THOU ART THE ONE:
THOU ART THY FATHER'S ONLY SONN!
TURN YEE BACK TO WHENCE YE CAME,
AND PUNISH THOSE AS ARE TO BLAME!

Look in Fengo's eye. You'll see the truth.
Look into your heart, boy. You'll see the truth.

Avenge this Murder. Slay thy Wicked Uncle.
Rise, rise to conquer Denn-Mark!

HORVENDAL　Please go back in the lake, father.

GHOST　Take my hand.

HORVENDAL　Please, father...no, father—

GHOST　TAKE THY FATHER'S HAND!!

HORVENDAL　Mercy...

GHOST　(*very softly*) Hooorvendaaal...Brave Horvendaall...
Revenge...Revenge....

HORVENDAL　Nooooo!!

*The GHOST kisses his hand. HORVENDAL is
seized with a deathly shiver.*

GHOST   Revenge, Horvendal, Revenge!
Remember me...Remember me...
Horvendaaaal...Remember me....

> *The GHOST vanishes. HORVENDAL is alone.*
> *Long silence.*

HORVENDAL   Jesus, if you got somethin to say, you better say it right now...

> *Pause. A wolf howls.*

HORVENDAL   OH HELL!

I must return — the Truth to know. Oh SPITE!
Why will no one tell me what is right?

> *He staggers home.*

***

Scene The Fifth

FENGO's house. Breakfast.

*Vikings guard the door. FENGO and
MATTHIUS sit by the fire, sharing a jug of ale.*

FENGO	Ha haaaaaa! Have another splodge.
MATTHIUS	Yer my best pal.
FENGO	I know.
MATTHIUS	Yer my best, best pal.
FENGO	Yer my pal too, Matthius.
MATTHIUS	Friends is a rare commodity. Yuz gots t'hang on to the few yuz gots Fengo, and cherish them and give them gifts.
FENGO	Don't fret, Matthius, I cherish your friendship.
MATTHIUS	You and me we go waay back. Why, I was takin flak fer yer pranks when we was brats plus I bloody well helped ye slay yer brother dint I?
FENGO	Yer a good egg, Matthius.
MATTHIUS	You knows I am, Fengo, you better knows I am. You owes me a big reward.
FENGO	You'll get what you deserve.

MATTHIUS	Election's acomin. The Freeman's Assembly. Seven more years we'll make'm buggers vote you.
FENGO	And so they will Matthius, so they will — if you remember to keep yer trap shutt.
MATTHIUS	And what does that mean?
FENGO	You know exactly what that means. They votes for Fengo, Matthius, they votes for gutts, soliditie. You don't go braggin, Matthius, 'bout brother-killing!
MATTHIUS	Are you implyin—
FENGO	I'm not implying it. I'm saying it. Keep yer stupid fat mouth shut. You never know when to shut up, Matthius. Plus yer always kissin my arse.
MATTHIUS	But—
FENGO	It looks peculiar. Stop it. At least when we're in public, you understand?
MATTHIUS	I'm sorry, Fengo.

A cry from outside.

GERUTHA	Fengo! Fengo!
FENGO	What's that?

GERUTHA rushes in.

GERUTHA	My boy, my boy!
FENGO	What's this? Yer boy? Yer boy what's banishd? What's he done this time, is he dead?
GERUTHA	They found him Fengo, somethin's happened to my boy. They found him starvin, lyin naked in the snow!

FENGO   Haa! Good!

GERUTHA   My boy! Frozen and brainsick!
Please let him into the house, Fengo — look at him.

FENGO   No! Fengo has spoken.

GERUTHA   Husband, mercie! Fatherly mercie!
He int no hindrance to no one no more!
He int no Christian, he int much of anything,
My boy, he's — look, Fengo, look!

> *Enter Vikings carrying THE MAD BOY, mad
> and soiled, wrapped in a blanket. He is drooling.*

HORVENDAL   Brrrr....

GERUTHA   They found him, Fengo, barking and ahowling —
chasing the thralls around, snarling and biting their
feet.

FENGO   Well I'll be.

HORVENDAL   Mommie—

FENGO   This is got to be some kind of joke. Here, why are
you barkin and aslobberin like a hound, kidda? Look
what yer doin to yer poor softhearted Maa.

GERUTHA   My child, my only child—

FENGO   He just don't wanna be banish'd! Let him go, woman.
I said let him go! Menn, toss this Mad Boy back out
in the snow. Nice try, kidda.

> *The vikings drag him out.*

GERUTHA   WHAT? No, Fengo. STOP! I'll nott— I'll *nott* allow
this!

FENGO   What?

GERUTHA   Can't you see what your hardness has done to him?
             Do you not think that this is enough?

FENGO   No.

GERUTHA   Is there no end to yer ignorance, Fengo?

FENGO   Are you sayin there should be?

GERUTHA   Look at the boy, Fengo—

FENGO   He's shamming! I pulled this trick once meself! No,
             woman, Fengo knows best. I know this kid better
             than you.

GERUTHA   When will it end, Fengo? When will yer crueltie end?
             When I'm dead, when he's dead, when you've driven
             all of us madd? When will you be happy? What're
             you tryin to prove? You bloody, thick, horrible —
             Coward!

FENGO   What did you say?

MATTHIUS   Don't take that from her Fengo.

FENGO   Matthius shut up. What did you say to me?

GERUTHA   Coward, Fengo, Coward. Coward! What else befits
             yer deeds?
             What sort of Chieftain'd freeze a Madd Boy to death?
             What sort of Chieftain bee you?
             Earth and heaven! You think the Godds be blind?
             You think the people Fengo can't suss out
             The reasons why you hate this boy?
             Someday, someways, your deeds will come to light;
             And when they do, Fengo, no more laughing.
             They'll haul you upp afore the High Assembly,
             Vote you down, and take yer goods away!

GERUTHA (*continued*) Annul our marriage, cast you outt.
Disgrace and shame will rain upon your head!
Coward, Fengo! Coward still I say!
All the world will see you and agree;
So cast us out, kill the boy — who cares?
Let the Heavens judge what Mann you be.

Long pause. He glares at her.

FENGO Oh woman, your mouth.

MATTHIUS Sod the heavens, Fengo, kill'im anyway.

FENGO Matthius, I thought I told you to shut up,

Pause. The Vikings look at him.

Alright, womann. You can keep yer Madd Boy.
But ye gots to keep him tied up, understand?

GERUTHA Do ye hear that, sonn?

FENGO And if he turns out to be ashammin, my dear,
I'll take you, and yer Madd Boy —
And naill youz both — to that WALL.
Go on. Tie him up out in the yard.

GERUTHA Horvendal, sweetheart, you're home.

FENGO Don't say I never done nothin for ye.

*Vikings carry THE MAD BOY out. GERUTHA
follows.*

MATTHIUS Mark my words.

FENGO I'll mark yer face in a second.

MATTHIUS Yer losin yer power, Fengo. I see it comin. Yer
waffling ways will ruin you. Yer doomed.

FENGO   Shut up, Matthius.

MATTHIUS   You'll rue the day, Fengo, you'll rue the day
                forever—

FENGO   Shut up, Matthius. Shut up, shut up!

> *They exit. Pause. Meanwhile. THE MAD BOY
> is tied up and left alone. He smears himself with
> ashes. Drums sound. He speaks.*

HORVENDAL   So here I sit, a stormtoss'd ladd
                Who once was sane, and now is madd;
                And all my foes what pressd me down
                Are helpless gainst me, standing round!
                Now I has him! Now he's mine!
                Now I've got him, by the spine!
                Horvendal who out was flung,
                Has gott you, Fengo, by the tongue!
                For doggs have ears and fools have eyes,
            →   That see men's secrets, hear through lies.
                I'll catch those lies, and when I do,
                I'll stain the earth with Fengo's grue!
                But is this mine — this Heart of Hate?
                Is this my Path? Is this my Fate?
                Oh hide, my witts, till all I see;
                Till then, a Madd Boy must I be!
                I'll hound these Fates out — wait and see.
                Till then, a Madd Boy must I be...

> *Drums rise. He rolls in filth and ashes.*

***

Scene The Sixth

The north shore. Morning. Calm.

*The old sisters sing an ancient mournful song.
LILJA sits and watches them repairing a fishing
net. She stares at the horizon.*

LILJA   Oh Inga, which way is south?

INGA   South, girl? Why, that way I believe.

LILJA   Is it true what they say, Inga? There's a land to the
South where it's summer all the time? And the
Birdsn' the Fishn' the Animals can talk? And nobody
ever fights no one ever, cause everybody is best
friends?

INGA   So I heard tell, girl, so I heard tell.

LILJA   How far a walk is it, Inga?

INGA   Too far for a little one like you.

LILJA   Ohhh. That's where he was goin. Fengo's foster-son,
the Young Horvendal. But now he's gone mad they
say. Out of his head! Just think of it, Inga, Madd!

INGA   Child, yer a born romantic.

LILJA   He used to talk of a godd called — Jesus. What was
he the godd of, Inga?

INGA   Jesus? From what I hear — he's the god of being

LILJA   Crucified! Crucified! I think — I'd like to be
     Crucified!

INGA   I'm tryin to do me chores, child. Stop yer yappin.

LILJA   Is it true what they say, Inga? Jesus is acomin to save
     us? That the high shall be made low and the low shall
     be made high and the wicked shall be driven hence and
     the good and virtuous shall prevail?

INGA   Cah! What say you? What topsyturvy drivel is that?

LILJA   That's what the Angell said, Inga, last night. He came
     again to my bed.

INGA   Angels, angels, yer always seein angels.
     Child yer a pain up the hole.

LILJA   Oooh Inga, I wish I could go southways. Anywhere,
     anywhere away from Denn-Mark.

INGA   Child there int nothin outside o' Denn-Mark, 'cept
     Wolves perhaps. And Snakes. And Black-Menn.

LILJA   Wolves and Snakes and Black-Menn! Just think!

INGA   Girl, you got a death-wish.

     The women leave. LILJA stays.

LILJA   Ocean, blue ocean, you wrench the yearnings from
     my heart;
     Tell me you spirits — tell me where to start!

***

Scene The Seventh

Night. FENGO and GERUTHA's bed.

HORVENDAL lies at the foot of the bed like a dog. Viking guards loom outside the door.

FENGO Roll over woman, Fengo wants a shag.

GERUTHA No.

FENGO I beg yer pardon?

GERUTHA Not with him in the bed.

FENGO I said love me, mother—

GERUTHA Get yer paws off me!

FENGO That does it, that's it! By the Lord o' Thunder, by the Lord o' the Slain, that does it. I'm kickin him out—

GERUTHA Don't touch that boy, Fengo! I said, don't touch that boy! It's cold outside. He's sleepin in here.

    Pause.

FENGO Ahh! Well, here's a fine how do ye do.
A Madd Boy sleepin in Fengo's bedd.

HORVENDAL Cuddle me, Dadda.

FENGO Get off me!

GERUTHA   Oh Horvendal, sweet Horvendal, tell us your woes.

HORVENDAL   Mother is that you? What happened to my brain?

GERUTHA   Oh, I don't know.

HORVENDAL   Me father, where's me father?

GERUTHA   You know where he is, son. He's dead, dead these seven years.

HORVENDAL   Oh Father, dead Father, how I miss him. I am so sadd.

FENGO   Sadd my arse. Yer Daddy was a cockswipe. Laddie when yer paa was alive he used to bind you and make you pull his sled.

HORVENDAL   How did ye come lord, Fengo?

FENGO   What?

HORVENDAL   How did my dead Dadda die?
Was it Trolls, Momma, done hauld him away?
Or was it Gnomes, Momma, spirited him off?
Or were it somethin else, Momma? Somethin green and meaner?
Somethin fatt and foul and furry — with one eye?

FENGO   Woman...

GERUTHA   You know how he died, son, everyone knows —
Struck down by a roaring thunderbolt — I mean...

HORVENDAL   That int what the birds told us.

GERUTHA   What?

HORVENDAL   That int what the birds told Mad Boy...

GERUTHA   Horvendal, sweet son, birds can't tell you nothin.
           That's just yer madness, chirpin in yer head.

HORVENDAL Chirp chirp.

GERUTHA   Now please, please get ye to sleep. Oh sleepy, happy
           family, we three.

           Pause.

FENGO   What did the birds tell you, Mad Boy?

GERUTHA   Please, Fengo—

FENGO   What's all this yer sayin about birds?

HORVENDAL I don't remember.

FENGO   Don't you be shittin me, sonn. Look me i' the face.
           What did these birds tell you — about Fengo?

           Pause. HORVENDAL squeezes FENGO's nose.

HORVENDAL Honk honk.

FENGO   I want him out of here.

GERUTHA   Fengo!

FENGO   I want him OUT OF HERE! NOW!

GERUTHA   I'the name o' heaven, i'the name o'the godds,
           He don't know what he sayin, Fengo — he's turn'd
           simple!

FENGO   That little bastard, that little titt-clutcher, he's turnin
           mee simple too! Barking, snarling, mewling
           babytalk, hurling snivvling slanders in my house—

           FENGO looks right at him.

FENGO
He better pray to Jesus he is a simpleton. He better pray he don't know what he's sayin. Cause if I finds out he *do* know what he's sayin — I'll have his gutts thru his nose. You understand that, sonn? Do ye?

GERUTHA
Fengo, stop!

FENGO
Listen, sonn — I never touch'd yer Paa!
Whoever says I didd — is a dead man!

GERUTHA
Fengo! Stop! You're all riled up! You go take a walk till you're simmer'd down.

Pause.

FENGO
Ahhh woman. Ahhh the two of you!
Gimme more frikkin grief than the goutt.
Thank yer stars, woman, I int brash like my brother!
Then you'd weep. Then yer boy would howl.

He leaves. The Vikings still stand guard.
GERUTHA rocks HORVENDAL gently. Pause.

HORVENDAL
How did my Dadda die, Momma?

GERUTHA
Stop askin that.

HORVENDAL
Well how did he die?

GERUTHA
Quit askin me!

HORVENDAL
I love you, Mum.

GERUTHA
Ohhh my blisterd heart...
If only you knew. My poor poor Madd Boy...

She rocks him. Meanwhile. FENGO lurks
outside, sharpening his axe.

FENGO
So he has me. So he thinks.
Let him stalk me, like a Lynx!
Boy, you know not what you do:
Fengo's eye is watching you!
Greater foes have cross'd my path,
All were crush'd beneath my wrath;
Men of Chaos, Men of Warr,
Prov'd no match for Fengo's sword!
Now it's your turn — if you cann—
Hemi-semi-demi-Man!
Come and get me, Fengo's here—
I'll slit yer throat from Ear to Ear!
Watch me, stalk me, Eye to Eye,
One of us must blink — and die!
Stare me down, boy, just you try!
One of us must blink — and die!

***

Scene The Eighth

A wooded mountain. Late afternoon.

MATTHIUS and LILJA are hauling firewood.

MATTHIUS   Come on, girl, are ye good fer nothin?

LILJA   Yeah, yeah, Father, I'm tryin.

MATTHIUS   Tryin, tryin. Tryin my patience. If ye can't haul kindling girl, what'll become of ye? All the men in the community hate ye. They think yer odd.

LILJA sits down in the snow.

Alright, girl — alright, we'll rest. But when I was a lad they used to throw weaklings like you into the sea.

Ohh, don't fret, I don't mean to rail at ye. Someday, someway we'll find something yer good at. Be strong for yer poor dead Mother; take faith in the stars and the heavens. I do, for your sake, girl. The godds'd never craft ye for no cause.

Now then, rested enough. Much to be done, girl, firewood to haul. Gots to get homeways, backafore sundown. Come on! Come on then, child! You can do it! Pull!

Hoy — hoy — did you feel that?

LILJA   What, Father?

MATTHIUS	A wind! A warm wind out of nowhere.
LILJA	Aye.
MATTHIUS	You felt it too? A hot and swoltery wind? Tint right, girl — tint right. Tis not the time of year! There be it again! Feel ye it blow? What means this untimed current? I likes it not! Look, look child, look — the snow's aturnd to slush! That dead and dormant elm's asprouted leaves!
LILJA	Aye.
MATTHIUS	Turn ye back, turn ye back, We'll no part of mysteries and strangeness; tis not normal, girl, tis not for us! Nooo! (*looking* up) What's that in the sky? A sign, a fiery sign from Heaven!
LILJA	What is it, Paa?
MATTHIUS	Hide yer head—
LILJA	But what is it—
MATTHIUS	Hide away from it, girl! Let yer Father stand and ask its meaning. Obvious it wants to speak to mee!

He approaches cautiously.

What — in the name of the Valkyries — is that?

LILJA	Looks like a Cross, Father!
MATTHIUS	A what?
LILJA	I seen the Mad Boy wearin it. It's a Cross!
MATTHIUS	Not a Cross. Oh Filthy Retribution. Not a Cross! Not the Sign of Christ!

LILJA	Sign of Christ?
MATTHIUS	Ill Omen, ill Omen, this be it, this be it! Surely the Dark Times is come!
LILJA	What are you sayin, Father?
MATTHIUS	The Christians! Ohh they're a bloodthirsty tribe; They eats hot blood and they drinks mens' flesh! Plus they hangs folk, nails'em high on wooden posts! I seen sordid rendrins of it in their books!
LILJA	Didn't you slaughter a bunch of Christians once, Father?
MATTHIUS	SSSHHH child! Ssssh, they be alistening! They're comin! Comin to exact their revenge!

He freezes in horror.

Girl!

LILJA	What?
MATTHIUS	Yer hands — they're bleedin! Yer feet — yer feet — they're bleedin too!
LILJA	Wow.
MATTHIUS	Ohhh Lord Thunderhelm, now everythin makes sense— The signs are there for everyone to see! The Mad Boy feignin madness. Fengo, he's afloundering. Wimmen and children mouthin off to the menfolk — JESUS is coming!
LILJA	What?
MATTHIUS	FENGO! Laughed at me, did he? Fengo beware! Come on, girl! Save yourself! We're doomed!

LILJA   Father? Father? Father?

                 He runs back to the village. LILJA stays. Looks
                 at her bleeding hands. Licks them. Music. A
                 gentle voice speaks.

VOICE   Liljaa....

LILJA   Who's there?

VOICE   Liljaa...Liljaa...

LILJA   Who's there?

VOICE   Don't be afraid. Child, come closer.
                 Wonderful, wonderful news....

                 She follows.

                         ***

Scene The Ninth

Later. In front of FENGO's house.

MATTHIUS runs frantically into the village.

MATTHIUS   It's JESUS, Fengo! Jesus Lord of Christ!
He's acomin — stormin unto Denmark!

FENGO looks at him. The Vikings gather.

I seen his Cross, Fengo, blazin in the sky;
Jesus were snarlin, his tongue were made of fire;
And he sneakit up, behind me sweet and harmless daughter,
And slasht her wrists — with a Invisible Sword!

The Vikings gasp.

So there! There! I told ye from the beginning!
You kept snarking, 'Don't fear no God of Peace!'
I say fear him! Fear him! Lookit where we be!
Our home, our homestead is being invaded!

FENGO   You'd best be sure o' this Matthius.

*Enter GERUTHA with MAD BOY on a leash. MAD
BOY is wrapped in a soiled blanket. GERUTHA has
a wooden spoon and a bowl of gruel.*

MATTHIUS   Here he is now: aclingin to his Mummie.
He int no Madd Boy, Fengo, you'll see—

HORVENDAL   Woof woof.

MATTHIUS   He's a Christian Spy — a Christlie Ferret!
             Confess Mad Boy! Quit sniffin at me crotch!

HORVENDAL   Woof woof.

MATTHIUS   How come yer eatin that mouldy straw?

HORVENDAL   Helps digest the broken glass.

MATTHIUS   And why do you eat broken glass, Mad Boy?

HORVENDAL   Helps digest the stones.

MATTHIUS   Oh? And why do you eat stones?

HORVENDAL   Help digest sommet else.

MATTHIUS   Oh Mad Boy, and pray tell us what's that?

HORVENDAL   Come here Matthius, till I tells ye.

             MATTHIUS bends down. HORVENDAL grabs
             him by the ears. Bites his nose. Everyone
             laughs. MATTHIUS breaks free.

MATTHIUS   Aaaahh! Shut it, youz! This be Christian Treachorie!
             Here's the Meek, Fengo, come to seize the Earth!
             Look at him feigning, worming at our trustings—
             Here — what've you got inside in that blanket?

HORVENDAL   What?

             MATTHIUS fights with MAD BOY, tears open
             the blanket, discovers two huge iron fish-gaffs.

MATTHIUS   Haaa! What's this? What's this, Fengo? This and this?
             Fishgaffs, Fengo, swiped from off me shedd!
             This boy were gonna snag ye like a squid!
             Up, you weasel! You Christian Assassin,
             Yer no more a blessed fool than mee!

MATTHIUS	(*continued*) Heyup hearties, break his bones — Toss his bloody carcass in the Sea!

MATTHIUS and Vikings pummel HORVENDAL.

VIKINGS	RAAAHHH!!

GERUTHA dives into the midst of them. Beats the Vikings with her spoon. The Vikings scatter. Pause. GERUTHA defends HORVENDAL.

GERUTHA	DON'T ANY OF YOU touch my Madd Boy! Matthius, get yee away! The next one what touches my Madd Boy, He getts this spoon up his hole!

What sort of Norsemenn are you?
What sort of leader lets this pass?
Beatin on cripples, on poor defenseless children,
Blamin all yer paranoyicies on Christ!
I'm this Boy's Mother. I say let him be!
You want to scrapp with someone — scrapp with me!

It is written — on Odinn's Mighty Stone,
The Song of Havamal, which all of you should know—
That he who raises sword gainst fool or cripple
Is doomd to die a Coward's Death;
And never ever enter the Hero's Afterlife—
But suffer his victim's affliction — forever!
NOW which among you dares persecute this Mad Boy?
Shame upon you! Shame upon you all.

HORVENDAL	Woof woof.

Pause.

VIKING 1	She's right, Fengo. The wailin woman's right.
VIKING 2	Aye. Live ye, and live unharmed, Madd Boy.

VIKING 1	So long as this boy's madd, we'll not scratch him, Fengo.
	Shame on you, Matthius.
VIKINGS	Aye Coward! Shame! Shame on you!
MATTHIUS	What? But he's shammin! Fengo, call them back!
	Lads, come back here! Look see—

The Vikings walk away. Pause.

FENGO	Ain't you shamed of yourself?
MATTHIUS	What?
FENGO	Ain't you shamed of what you've said?
	Get down, Matthius, thank this goodly womann
	What spared you a fate worse than death.
MATTHIUS	What're you sayin?
FENGO	Matthius—
MATTHIUS	She's conspirin with him too! My friend, my cohort, after all our schemes and preparation — to be undone by a Christian — a beardless puling boy — the very sonn of the mann we...er...that is to say we — I...
FENGO	Matthius—

*He draws his knife and points it at him.
HORVENDAL is watching them, sucking his
little finger.*

Matthius. Get yerself home.
I'll talk to you later, Matthius.
Fengo is at the helm.

*MATTHIUS salutes and exits. FENGO watches
GERUTHA who comforts THE MAD BOY.*

GERUTHA   Why, why, does vileness beget vileness?
When, when, will patience beget peace?
Be it us, Fengo — be it us the Nordic wimmenfolk?
Ist somethin in what we do, or say, or don't say,
That makes you think we love your Blood-feuds?
We don't Fengo! Look at us! We don't!
See our tears, Fengo, follow to their source...

FENGO   Ohhh straind Gerutha, paragon of womanhood.
What a rack this plight of yours must be!
Faithful wife, loving mother, honourable, brave:
Sometimes woman, I think yer too good for this
world.

GERUTHA   No I ain't.

FENGO   Course you is! It's writt for all to see.
You liv'd a hard hard cruel life full o pain and tragedie.
Why don't you let Fengo make it up to you, hey?
Why don't you let Fengo babysitt the boy?

GERUTHA   I don't trust you.

FENGO   Fengo's changing!
Fengo's sorry he railed at you before.
There, there.

He hugs her. She sobs.

GERUTHA   Ohh if only I could start my life again.
If only I could turn around and change the past.

FENGO catches HORVENDAL's eye.

FENGO   Now, now, mousie, no use recountin the mucky
details.
What's done is done and can't be done again.
Bedways now. Tis past the Madd Boy's napp.
He'll be safe out here tonight, Mother, nae fear.

GERUTHA   Oh my poor, poor Madd Boy...

> *She kisses him and exits. FENGO ties HORVENDAL to a post.*

FENGO   Peace my boy, my bonnie ladd;
                  May all yer dreams be sweet, not sadd.
                  Fengo loves ye, this is true,
                  He wouldna' dream o' harmin you!
                  And so goodnight sweet boy goodnight,
                  May heaven shield ye in yer plight;
                  And if ye die, afore ye wake—

> *He kisses him on the forehead.*

Pray you do, for your own sake.

> *Music. FENGO leaves him. Transition into night. Wolves howl.*

***

Scene the Tenth

That night. Colder. Outside FENGO's house.

Silence. HORVENDAL is tied up, listening at the door. Out of the dark forest, LILJA emerges. She kneels in front of him. Pause.

LILJA
You're the Madd Boy. Hello, Madd Boy.
Don't be afraid. It's me, Matthius' daughter.
I come to bring you a message:

I seen this fella. A fella in the woods;
Small he was, beak-nosed and raven-hair'd,
Dark his face was, brambles on his head,
He said, my child, be ye not afraid.
To Horvendal I bring this Holy Plea,
To Horvendal I issue this decree:
Fly he says, get out this bitter land,
Or else another Fengo you'll become!
Then he wept, wept for vents unfolding,
Still he wept, questing where to turn,
Still he wept, blood come from his eyes,
Then he disappeared, into the drifting snow...

Twas Jesus, Madd Boy. Jesus spake your name!
Jesus calls you, Pilgrim to his Shrine!
I'm agoin — goin where he says,
To this city, place call'd — Jerusalem.
He calls ye, Mad Boy, back unto his fold;
He sent mee, Mad Boy, to save your tortur'd soul!

HORVENDAL What?

LILJA   Believe it—

HORVENDAL   Who put that in yer head?
                 Get yee back to girlie-land afore ye winds up dead!

                 She reaches into her cloak.

LILJA   No. I'll nott.
                 He told me you would doubt.
                 He told me show you this. He took it from his brow.
                 A Crown of Brambles — a helmet of pain,
                 He bore for love of us upon the Cross!
                 He left his bloody markings on me too;
                 On me hands, and on me feet. See?
                 He baptis'd me; annointed me; rockt me with such
                 shivers!
                 Vaulted me up, and show'd to me — such things!
                 He listens Mad Boy! He asks of you, believe!
                 Look you, his Love-Wounds!
                 Now — do you believe?

                 *Pause. He takes the crown of thorns. He looks at
                 her with tears in his eyes.*

HORVENDAL   Who are you?

LILJA   Who are you?

HORVENDAL   Are you an Angel?

LILJA   Are you?
                 Why Angel why, do break you Jesus' heart?
                 Why Angel why, do feign you like yer madd?

HORVENDAL   Oh GODDS! Oh girl, all I see is Fengo!
                 All muckt upp am I, adrowning in the murk!
                 I feel no Love, I see no Angels —help me!
                 Where was Jesus when I calld out his name?

LILJA   Maybe Mad Boy, you int listning hard enough.
                 Maybe Jesus is talking to you now.
                 Think of it Mad Boy! Run away with me!
                 Together out of Denn-Mark. Forever to be free!

HORVENDAL   Oh girl, girl, girl—

                 They embrace. Pause.

MATTHIUS   (*off*) Liljaaaa!

LILJA   Oh no—

MATTHIUS   (*off*) Girl, what are you doing? Heeyup! Come inside!

LILJA   I wait for you, Mad Boy, I pray for you.

HORVENDAL   But—

                 She kisses him. MATTHIUS comes out.

MATTHIUS   LILJAAAA!!!

LILJA   Runn — runn — with mee!

                 MATTHIUS grabs her, hauls her inside.
                 HORVENDAL is stunned. He looks at the crown
                 of thorns. Pause. Wolves watch HORVENDAL
                 from the woods.

HORVENDAL   Is this Madness makes me sit here thus?
                 Is this Madness beckons me to runn?
                 Why, Horvendal, do these godds torment ye,
                 Sending out their dictums in bits and fits and starts?
                 Oh Girl! Oh Girl! You rip my heart in twainn!
                 Ohhhh, throw away the weaker half—
                 And let — the Strong remain...

WOLVES   (*whispering*) Hooorvendaaaal....REVENNNGE....

        THE MAD BOY grinds the crown of thorns on his face.

            ***

Scene Eleventh

Next morning. The Woods. Behind the stables.

Dreadful screaming. FENGO, MATTHIUS and Vikings drag LILJA through the snow.

LILJA   OWWW! Let go!!!

FENGO   Further out—

LILJA   Let go! OOWWW!!! HEEELPP!!

FENGO   Matthius hold her firm.

LILJA   OOOWWWW!!!

MATTHIUS   What said he, girl? Fess up, we heard you!
               What said you to Mad Boy lurking by last night?

LILJA   Nothing, Paa!

MATTHIUS   We know yer in league with him.

LILJA   I'm not! I'm NOT!

FENGO   Matthius, wrench it out.

MATTHIUS   Something's between you. Something dark, unDanely.
               Say it, girl! This raiding spirit's took you both!

LILJA   OOOWWW!! It has not!

FENGO   She's shy. She needs prompting.
                 Hoist her smock Matthius, let her taste my belt.

MATTHIUS   NO! Fengo. NO! Please — no more floggings—
                 Faith, hear me, we'll chart the slyer way!
                 Crafticall — tackticall — like the Mad Boy himself!
                 A trapp then — to flush this marmott from his hole!

FENGO   Well?

MATTHIUS   Bind the girl, Fengo — leave her here alone,
                 Haul out the Mad Boy, let him glimpse her tied;
                 If he dare collude with her — if he move to free her —
                 If he dare unbind her, Fengo — then we have our Boy!

FENGO   It's a stupid plan.

MATTHIUS   Trust in mee!
                 If this plott mislay — let I horsewhippt be!
                 If he dare save her, Fengo, then he's no Madd Boy!
                 If he's no Madd Boy — then he's ours to slay.

FENGO   Hmmm. Alright Matthius try it. Bind her wrists.
                 And not kindlie, Matthius, not fatherly—
                 Harshly. Make it hurt!

                 They tie her wrists to the rail.

LILJA   OOOWW!!!

MATTHIUS   Oh wicked, wicked, wretched, weasling girl,
                 Look at me! Drove to bind you to a rail.

FENGO   Enough Matthius. Menn, fetch the Madd Boy.
                 Bide this plodger, let his tact be tried.
                 Meanwise, hide we in yonder spracky thicket—
                 Swords drawn, ladds! This lass we'll leave exposed.

                 The Vikings exit.

FENGO	Your final chance, Matthius. Tread ye slithe. Your worth to me is wayning. Fumble not.
MATTHIUS	He'll take her, Fengo, upon my throat he shall. If there's one thing Christian boys like to do, Fengo— It's abducting and corrupting little girls.
FENGO	Hmm.

Pause. Vikings enter with MAD BOY.

VIKING	Here's the boy, Fengo.
FENGO	Madd Boy! How slept you last night?
HORVENDAL	Arf arf!

FENGO holds him by the hair.

FENGO	Ahhh good Mad Boy, barkier than ever. Look Mad Boy. Quitt chewing of that logg. See ladd, see how Fengo trusts ye? He's found a task for yee, doggyskull'd or nott. This girl boundup — she's spoutin mouthy insolence. We'll just off to carve a slicing switch. Keep the watch on her, Mad Boy, see she don't get free. If she hollers, snapp her toes off — Snapp her ears off! Got it?
HORVENDAL	Arf arf arf!
FENGO	Matthius, come away. Be good, Mad Boy. Fearless Mad Boy. Peerless Madd Boy. Stay.

FENGO nods at the Vikings. They head off into the woods. HORVENDAL and LILJA are alone. Pause.

LILJA	Madd Boy listen — quickly now and hear—
HORVENDAL	Girl, what's happened??
LILJA	Ohhh, what a plundring's here! Boundup, battered on — all for my Angell! Battered by our Fathers — battered for my Christ!
HORVENDAL	I'm yours, girl! Tell me the Path this boy's to take; I heed you, love you! We runn for Jesus' sake.
LILJA	Naay — all's changed now! Christ he speaks afresh. Nay come not near, they're watching with their swords!
HORVENDAL	What? Where?
LILJA	Look not behind— It's you they're trappling, worry not for mee. It's you, Christ, he beckons! Hark! He bidds you now. Fly! Flee this trapp! Fly this place! Alone!
HORVENDAL	Alone?
LILJA	Now! Let Jesus guide your heels! Leave me to bleed, love! Give my love to Christ.
HORVENDAL	What? Leave you? Christ — bids you say this? Christ — he bids me leave you bleed alone? Christ — he bids me strand you with your fathers? Ye take this from yer menn, girl? Ye take this from yer Godd? Look at you!
LILJA	Doubt him nott!
HORVENDAL	*Make him help us*, you says he thrives in you! Jesus hear us — show your bloody love-strength! Off yer cross Christ, do yer Christly jobb! Jesus?

LILJA   Peace, love, peace. My time is over.
Your Star is risen, Angel. Rise! Shine on!

HORVENDAL   Noo! Ohh no. Murder's in the Stars.
Now more than ever do I my tactick see;
Christ — he's no Saviour! Christ — he's asleep!
Tis Thorr what beckons! Tis Thorr what thrives in
mee!

LILJA   No! No!

HORVENDAL   Hush, lass — it's true!
In Thorr do I flourish! This oath I swear to you:
When next we meet, yer plight will ended be,
And Fengo's head I'll naill on yonder tree!
Death to our Fathers!

LILJA   Take nott the course of Wrath —
Peace! Peace! Take not the course of Doom!

HORVENDAL   Enough!

LILJA   Oh Jesus, guide this boy with fire;
Help! We lose him! Oh slaughterous desire —
Pray with me, Mad Boy — praying let us die!
Aye! Let us fly this Earth! Die! Die!
Drown, in a Bloodbath of Love!
WE HEED YOU CHRIST!

HORVENDAL   Stop it!

LILJA   CHRIST, TAKE OUR SOULLS!
Adds two more to your martyrd litany!
Fathers, come forth! Come slay your Christian
Children!
We defy you, DEFY YOU IN THE NAME OF
CHRIST!!
PRAISE GODD!!

HORVENDAL   You'll kill us!

MATTHIUS   We have him, Fengo!
           Hah hurraah!! Forward axemenn!

           MATTHIUS runs out, followed by Vikings.

HORVENDAL Nooo! Squalling lass! Not Christians! Not Christ!
           No! Stop! I'm a mangling Madd Boy—

           He bites off her ear.

LILJA   OOOOOOOWW!!

           He runs home howling.

MATTHIUS   After him men, after him, after him—

           The Vikings follow.

FENGO   Well, Matthius, there's your craftick plann.

MATTHIUS   Did he try to free you, did he try to cutt yer bonds?
           Thor's hounds, Fengo, he's chaw'd off her ear!

FENGO   So he has.

LILJA   Jesus, take me, take me from this land...
           In the name of love, in the name of heavenmercie,
           Someone, anyone, anyone, let me die...

           She sobs, bleeding.

MATTHIUS   Girl, what's got into you?

FENGO   Matthius, this was your last chance.
           You have wasted countless hours of my life.
           From this time henceforth, let our paths turn twain.
           Come not to my house, come not to my table,
           I'm done with ye, Matthius, I renounce yee!

           He tears off MATTHIUS' medallions.

MATTHIUS	What? No! Fengo, Fengo noooo— My bloodiest blood brother, give me one last chance.
FENGO	Let go of me, Matthius. You int no Viking, nor no Dane.
MATTHIUS	I am, I am! I'm trying— I'll show you—
FENGO	Matthius — go play dolls with yer daughter.

He spits on MATTHIUS and strides away. MATTHIUS kneels with his head in his hands, sobbing.

MATTHIUS	Ohh noo, ohh Fengo, ohh Odinn, what'll come of me, I'm done for...

LILJA talks to herself.

LILJA	My fault, my fault. This is all my fault... No faith, no hope, no courage...I failed...
MATTHIUS	Aye, that's it — you failed — yer hopeless! Inside, you hopeless thing.
LILJA	But—
MATTHIUS	Inside! Get ye inside now!

He unties her, shoves her homeward. Elsewhere, MAD BOY jumps on FENGO's back.

HORVENDAL	Piggyback, Nuncle Fengo — piggyback, piggyback!
FENGO	Lad, get down afore ye breaks yer neck.

The Vikings hold him.

HORVENDAL	I did like ye said, Nuncle, I snappt at her ear!

FENGO   Aye for that, we'll bedd you in the shedd.

HORVENDAL   Ooh! What funn was today, Nuncle Fengo!

FENGO   Aye. Bind him good.
What a frolick we'll have the morrow.

> *The Vikings bind him firmly in the woodshed.*
> *FENGO speaks aside.*

FENGO   Oh canny, canny Madd Boy; thou'rt indeed the one.
The game it is afoot kidd; thou art thy Father's Sonn.

> *They leave him in the shed. The Vikings stand*
> *watch. Elsewhere, LILJA lies weeping in her*
> *bed.*

***

Twelfth Scene

That sleepless night. MATTHIUS's house.

MATTHIUS and LILJA lie awake. LILJA nurses her wound. Pause.

LILJA   Dadda?

MATTHIUS   What, girl?

LILJA   Why was I born?

MATTHIUS   Because, girl, because.

LILJA   It ain't fair.

MATTHIUS   Go to sleep.

LILJA   Dadda?

MATTHIUS   What, girl?

LILJA   How come I'm me?

MATTHIUS   Shut up.

LILJA   I don't want to be alive. I want to be dead.

MATTHIUS   Well yer not, girl. Yer alive. If everyone was dead—
Well...there'd be no point to life, would there?

LILJA   It ain't fair.

MATTHIUS   Go to sleep.

Pause

LILJA   I tried, I tried! Oh Jesus where were you?
I saw you, I dream'd you. I can't reach you no more.

Pause.

Dadda?

MATTHIUS   What, girl?

LILJA   I want to kill myself.

MATTHIUS   Oh stop it.

LILJA   I am gonna kill myself, Da. I want to die.

MATTHIUS   Suicide's fer menn, child. It's a honourable death. You
coudnt kill yerself any mor'n a dog could. Now get to
sleep.

LILJA   Says you.

MATTHIUS   Says me.
I wish you would kill yerself, if the truth be told.

LILJA   I'll do it, Da.

MATTHIUS   Good. Join yer Mother.

LILJA   I mean it. I'll jump off a cliff.

MATTHIUS   Good! Here, Take my dagger with you, slit yer throat on
the way down. Here — take me bloody warr-axe too —
chop yer own head off while yer at it. Well? Go on!
What're you waitin for? Go on!

LILJA   I don't think you're a very good father.

MATTHIUS Well, whose fault is that? Not mine.
Think I'm hard on ye, girl? Go and face the godds.
Think this world's cruel? Go and try the next!
Go on! Ye got yer axe, ye got yer dagger.
Go on — quit stallin — go do yerself in.

> *She stands there a while, looking at the axe,*
> *patricide flashing through her mind.*
> *At the same moment, in FENGO's bed,*
> *GERUTHA jumps up from her sleep.*

GERUTHA AAAH!

> *LILJA drops the axe and throws her arms around*
> *MATTHIUS, weeping.*

MATTHIUS What's this? How come yer huggin mee?

LILJA I love you, Dad. I don't care what you are. I don't
want to die — I want to live — I want to live — I
want to live...

MATTHIUS Then get to sleep.

> *Meanwhile:*

GERUTHA I seen her, Fengo, I seen her in a dream;
Her smock, the hue of deepest bluest sky;
She look'd at me, like sunlight did she seem,
And Love and Mercie nested in her eye;
"Gerutha," call'd she — call'd me by my name.
Told me my misdoings were forgott;
No one ever looked at me the same,
And lov'd me so, if I lov'd her or nott!
She's comin, Fengo, comin to this Land,
She and her Sonn, who some call Jesus Christ.
And all of Denn-Mark will take her by the hand,
And Light will shine, where only there was ice!
I seen it, Fengo — I seen it clear as day!
The Morning's come. Our sinns are wash'd away.

FENGO gets out of bed.

FENGO

That does it, that's it,
I ain't sleepin with no crazywoman.
You been eatin rancid bugberries, that's your problem.
So now — Jesus Christ is got a mother...

*At the same moment. HORVENDAL dreams. A
strange voice whispers. It sounds like LILJA.*

LILJA

Horvendal? Horvendal? Where is my Love?

HORVENDAL

Who's that?

LILJA

Are you awake, Horvendal? Let me in.

HORVENDAL

Lilja? Girl?

LILJA

Aye love it's mee—
I come to gett you — together let's flee.

HORVENDAL

Girl, forgive me!

LILJA

Shhh...open the door!
Take me and heed me, as ye should've before—

HORVENDAL

I do, girl, I loves you!

LILJA

I loves ye too.

HORVENDAL

If only the godds were hearted, as you!

*He goes to the door and opens it. A bolt of light.
The GHOST of Horvendal the Elder is there
instead.*

GHOST

Hooorvendaaal. Hooorvendaaal. Revenge!!

HORVENDAL

No, Dadda—

GHOST　　　　Revenge Revenge Revenge Revenge!!

HORVENDAL　No, Dadda — no, Dadda — no---

　　　　　　　　He slams the door.

　　　　　　　　Hoy shite.

　　　　　　　　Meanwhile. Outside. FENGO looks at the moon.

FENGO　　　　Odinn, Great Odinn, speak ye to Fengo.
　　　　　　　　It's mee, yer old warrior, steadfast and true;
　　　　　　　　Who is this Lord Jesus? What does he want?
　　　　　　　　Why ain't I seen him — or even seen you?
　　　　　　　　Great Odinn — wisen me. Show me what to do.
　　　　　　　　Faill me nott — or I'll wage Warr on you!

　　　　　　　　Drums sound. Wolves whisper in the shadows.

WOLVES　　　Reveeeenge...

　　　　　　　　　　***

Thirteenth Scene

Early morning. The coast. High wind.
A remote hill overlooking the sea.

Enter FENGO singing, THE MAD BOY led by
Vikings. They rest. FENGO waits. Slowly, the
Viking guards leave.

FENGO   Look, Mad Boy. Look out at the Sea.
Don't it bestirr yer blood? It stirs mine.
Come closer, lad. Look back at the valley.
See; what a beautiful land we live in.

You know lad: the poets, the ancient saga-writers,
They tell us Love's the mightiest thing on earth.
Dost believe that, son? Is't Love? Or is it Hate?
Can Love move a Mountain? Can Love win a Warr?
Can it, son? Hate can.

Witness us, us the Viking people:
Were't Love what made us rulers o' the world?
Were't Love what stood us up gainst Mother Nature's
blast?
Ohhhh Nature: from Time's Dawn she despised us.
We, her batter'd children, hated her right back.
See! how we battle her, since time immemorial,
But we're winning, boy; we're winning.
Praise our swords, we rise!

FENGO   (*continued*) Madd Boy, hear us.
Its tyme t'quitt yer shammin.
You int no Christian, nor no Fool.
All this Love talk, bout Jesus, bout Mary —
It's a plott to keep us Strongmen down!
And that ain't natural, sonn. It's perverse!
Skews the Fatal Majestie of Heaven!
Fengo won't have it.

Men of Greatness should brace themselves together,
Gainst the rising tide of mediocre muck.
Fear it, sonn, fear it — a world rul'd by weaklings —
We gotts to stick together, and stand tall.
Love sputts and flickers, a faint and fleeting fyrefly;
Hate will one day engulf the sunn!
Let not our Hates drive our hearts asunder,
But bond us, boy, bond us,
Meld our hearts with shining gold!
Give us your hand...

HORVENDAL   Gold?

FENGO   Aye, sonn — Gold!
Gold and Power, sonn. My second in command!
Clever Madd Boy! Thour't prov'd a cunning foe,
Try usin those skills — for something grander.

HORVENDAL   Yoooou — Coward Fengo!

FENGO   Laddie, watch what you say.
Fengo won't bargain, after today.

HORV   Coward! You Coward, Fengo! I've gott you by the throat!
You skulking sott to bribe me with yer Gold!
What hope has Denn-Mark if you're the best it's gott?
My Time is come! Yer bones are growing old.

FENGO   Ohhhh you said it. You gone and said it now.
                 I see yer Father — he's alivin in yer gutts.
                 Fengo's agonna have to prowse him out!

                 FENGO throws off his cloak.

                 Wrassle me, sonn. Let's do this honourable.
                 Fair and square, no dirty tricks allowd;
                 No henchmen here — no Mother do I see.
                 Just you and me, sonn. Do yer Father proud.

HORVENDAL   Did yee slay my Father?

FENGO   That ain't fer you to know.
                 Tear it fromm me, laddie. Give yer luck a go.

HORVENDAL   No weapons?

FENGO   No weapons.

HORVENDAL   Teeth and claws?

FENGO   Teeth and claws.
                 No, sonn, no trappings, no sneakrie, no bait.
                 Just you, boy, and me — and pure, unbridled Hate!

                 Pause. HORVENDAL takes off his cloak.

HORVENDAL   Strengthen me Godds!

FENGO   Ahhhhh. Christian my arse!
                 Now yer deepest hue shines! Welcome back.
                 Ready boy? Ready? Stay inside the clearing.
                 In Thorr's name face me. Brace me. Grasp hands.

HORVENDAL   May the best man winn.

FENGO   If he didn't winn he'd not be the best mann would he?
                 Now — on yer mark, get sett, GO!!

> *FENGO kicks him in the groin then grips him in a hammerlock.*

HORVENDAL Oooomph!

FENGO You puny thing!

HORVENDAL You bloody ox!

FENGO Surrender?

HORVENDAL Never, Fengo — don't relax yer gripp,
I'll grind yer grimy gullet wi' me teeth!

FENGO Heh heh, oohhh the memories they flood;
Yer Father was a hopeless fighter too!
No grace, the fucker used to bite and scratch!
Took all the funn out o' molestin him.

> *HORVENDAL tries to break free.*

HORVENDAL Ooomph!!

FENGO C'mon, laddie, try and throw me!

HORVENDAL Oomph!

FENGO How yuz doin, Madd Boy?

HORVENDAL Help!

FENGO Over the shoulder, Mad Boy, over the shoulder.
Come on, Madd Boy, you can do it, you can do it.
I know ye can — OOOMPH!

> *HORVENDAL flips FENGO over his shoulder
> and he lands with a colossal thud!*

Oooooooohhhh!

HORVENDAL	Haaa! Mad Boy's gott you now!
	Praise Ye, Lord Thunder! Where's yer bullytalk now?
FENGO	I can't breathe...
HORVENDAL	What?
FENGO	Me back — me back — it's broke...
HORVENDAL	What's this then, Fengo? A dagger in yer breeks?
	No dirty tricks you said! No dirty tricks!
FENGO	Help!
HORVENDAL	Now did yee slay my Father?
FENGO	Help!
HORVENDAL	You slew my Father dead!
FENGO	I never touch'd him! Someone, someone help!
	Yer facts are scrambled, Mad Boy, in yer head!
HORVENDAL	I *seen* you Fengo! I seen you break his skull.
	You never seen me hidin in that tree!
	Seven years me mind it did deny it.
	But it's back, Fengo! Me Father lives in mee!

HORVENDAL slices him across the scalp.

FENGO	AAAHHH!! Fuck me, you really are a Mad Boy!
	Deluded sick and bloodicrazed to boot!
	But as yer a mann, you'd best murder me quickly —
	To torture me would bring you no credit!
HORVENDAL	Oh noo, Fengo: I waited seven years!
	I'll mapp out the bounds of my Revenge.
FENGO	Heelp!!

HORVENDAL   And when you feel my steel cut yer hamstrings,
Remember the abuse you heap'd on me!

FENGO   NoooOOOO!!

HORVENDAL slices FENGO's hamstrings with his knife.

HORVENDAL   No, Uncle, no, yer life ain't over;
You got many many nastie hours ahead!
Move mann — I'll spear ye thru the heels
And hoist ye up for skinnin on that tree!
Move!

FENGO   JESUS, GOD OF MERCY hear my plea —
Deliver me from this Boy! JESUS! JESUS! —

HORVENDAL   Fucker can't hear ye!
Wait...what's that, what's here?

Pause. In the distance can be heard solemn singing.

Voices singing? Bronze bells ringing?
Friends o' yours, I fear!
No! It's Latin! No, it cannot be!
Someone's comin up the road!

FENGO   Let's see!

HORVENDAL   You be still! No! I'll not believe!
No it ain't — mine eyes — they be deceiv'd!

Enter a procession of travelling monks holding cowbells, crucifixes and holy relics. One of the monks, BROTHER PAAVO, steps forward and faces them.

PAAVO   Ahoy, you wild and woolie Heathen;
         Break off your squallid squabblings.
         We are sent from Jesus and the Pope,
         To seek the Lord of Helsingor!

HORVENDAL   Lord of Helsingor?

FENGO   I am he! I am he!
         I am Fengo, Lord of Helsingor. What can I do fer
         yee?

PAAVO   We carry a message from Rollo, King of Neustria.

FENGO   Rollo the Bald? What does he want?

PAAVO   An audience, Lord Fengo. An audience in private.
         An audience bearing matters of importt.

         Pause. He looks at HORVENDAL.

FENGO   A haudience. They request a haudience of me.
         Give us yer hand, good brother, I'm maimed.
         Sorry Madd Boy. Matters of State.
         We'll have to finish our conversation later!

HORVENDAL   No!

         The monks help FENGO up.

FENGO   Welcome all! Welcome to Helsingor! Land of heartie
         cheer!
         Bigg feastin and ale for Fengo and the Christians!
         This way, good strangers! This way!

         HORVENDAL is stunned.

HORVENDAL   Christians?

FENGO   Aye, son. Christians! Who knows why or how? Got you, Mad Boy, got you! Just watch what happens now.

                    The monks sing. They exit with FENGO. HORVENDAL stares after them.

HORVENDAL   Christians..? Christians..?

              Oh Christ!

                    End of Act One.

Act Two,
Fourteenth Scene

DRUMS. FENGO'S house at Helsingor.

*FENGO, GERUTHA, and Vikings sit facing the
Christians. The old women dress FENGO's
wounds. He laughs.*

FENGO   Well, well, well. Who woulda ever believ'd it.
Christian priests. In Helsingor.

PAAVO   Lord Fengo, I am Brother Paavo.
This good Holy Man, this is Brother Petri.

GERUTHA   Welcome, brothers—

FENGO   Mind yer business, womann —
Youz gots some nerve prancin across my land.

PETRI   We bear a message from Good King Rollo;
He'll stand your persecuting us no more.
Signed a treaty did he, with the French;
And in exchange for lands and yearly tribute,
Swore before God, Fengo — to make the Danes
Christian.

FENGO   Did he now?

PETRI   That means all his Lords, all his Vikings,
Every Danish fisherman and blacksmith,
Must awake, and heed the rising tide,
And join Christ's People by New Year's Day.

PAAVO	The One Thousanth Year of our Lord. Amen.
PETRI	Wilt thou, Fengo, staunch and stubborn savage, Take up the Cup of Jesus Christ? Or wilt thou stay, and keep your brutish ways, And face the wrath of Rollo, your superior?
FENGO	Hmm...
PAAVO	E'en as we speak, Fengo, Jesus Christ impends. His Knights of the Purple Cross sweep North; Lord Thorstalf, your neighbour, he refus'd our clerics; Lo and behold Fengo, his house burn'd down.
PETRI	Praise the Power of the Lord.
PAAVO	Speak, Fengo. Time's no longer with you. Fend us back, another wave will rise. We come to you, to offer you Salvation. Your answer now, directly. Speak!
FENGO	Hmmm...
GERUTHA	I dreamed, I dreamed this day was coming—
FENGO	Woman, I thought I told you to shut up.

Pause.

PAAVO	Well?
FENGO	Hmmm. Youz Christians, youz drives a hard bargain. King Rollo, he's a devious old foxx. Tell King Rollo —we accepts these prim conditions. Tell him — Fengo wants a slice!
PAAVO	Praise God.
FENGO	Show us yer book. Yer Jesus book. Now! I feels a strange new melting in my heart.

They open a huge bible.

PAAVO	Look you here — that's Tender Babie Jesus, And Mary his Mother, and good Saint Joseph, Riding on the Road to Bethlehem.
FENGO	I see.
PETRI.	And this is Jesus, all grown up now, All killed and Crucified, hanging on a Cross.
FENGO	I like that picture.
PAAVO	And here's Our Lord again, all Resurrected like. Rising into the sky, to join his Father in Heaven.
FENGO	Ahh...that's Beautiful. That's what that is. Poignant, Poetick and Beautiful, hey? More, more, tell me more about this! I can tells yer wise and goodlie menn.
PAAVO	Jesus said, love thine enemy as thyself.
FENGO	Aye, that'd throw'em!
PAAVO	He said, judge not, lest ye be judged.
FENGO	Aye, no judgin Fengo!
PETRI	Jesus said, verily, from the greatest to the smallest, We are all equal in the eyes of the Lord.
FENGO	Ahhhh...we're all equal. You hear that womann? Why that's lovlie! That's poetickal too.
GERUTHA	Amen.
FENGO	And if yuz do something badd an' yer sorry, Jesus will forgive ye, int that right?
PAAVO	Aye.

FENGO	Now, what if ye ain't sorry? What if yer proud? What if yer some bastard tryin to murder Fengo?
PAAVO	What?
FENGO	Punishments! Punishments! Yuz gotts t'have punishments, boys. What've ye gott?
PETRI	Why?
PAAVO	Penances, Fengo.
PETRI	Excommunication.
PAAVO	Depending on the Severity of the Sin.
FENGO	Dependin on the Severity — of Fengo. Ha haaaa!

Pause. The monks look at one another.

Well, good holymen, I likes yer words. I likes your books and I likes your pictures. Plus, we don't want to be left behind, right ladds? Don't want to stand i'the way of progress!

GERUTHA	But Fengo—
FENGO	Let the statues of Odinn be cut down, Let great crucifixes be erected in their stead! Tell yer Christian bosses Fengo wants aboard! Womann — yer the first heathen I'm hex-communicatin!
GERUTHA	What?
FENGO	So long — Mother o' the Madd Boy! Smell you in hell, woman! You boys drink ale?
PAAVO	Er...

FENGO Ale! Ale for my celibate friends!
Let the horn be sounded and the sheep slaughterd!
Rowse the musicians! Let the Festival begin!
Jesus is come to Helsingor!!

VIKINGS Hurraaaay!!

Music. Drums. FENGO rises on his crutches.
The Vikings cheer, douse the monks with ale.
The dragonhead posts outside FENGO's hall are
taken down, and hauled off to the lumberyard.

***

Fifteenth Scene

Down in the village. Later.

A Viking craftsman nails crossbeams on the dragonhead posts, to make them look like crosses. HORVENDAL and the old women watch.

HORVENDAL   Fengo a Christian? No, impossible!

INGA   Aye, he's gonna to be baptisd, Sunday morning!

ANNA   Baptis'd in the sea!

HORVENDAL   I was a Christian! I heard of Christ first!

INGA   Aye, he's going to confess his sinns afore the townsfolk.

ANNA   Aye and we'll confess too, and Fengo will absolve us!

INGA   Fengo says Jesus murders all sinners with a Hammer!

HORVENDAL   He *what*?

ANNA   Aye, I believe it — and Fengo said to mee—
That Jesus, he specially hates...old wimmen!

INGA   Oooh we better get baptised soon!

HORVENDAL Oh you Hound-Fates! Every turn is wrong!
Jesus, treachor-godd, spurn'd us all along!
Fengo's rook'd you! Christ, you took his side!
But I shall stitch my vengeance-capp with
Fengo's Danish hide.
Let him confess. The Baptism's the place,
Where I'll rubb Viking Justice in his Face!

***

Scene Sixteenth

The hall at Helsingor.

FENGO sits at his high seat. MATTHIUS enters sheepishly.

MATTHIUS   Fengo? Fengo?

FENGO   Matthius, yer hex-communicated.

MATTHIUS   I know, Fengo, I know. I...I got a surprise fer yee.

FENGO   Do you, Matthius?

MATTHIUS   I do indeed.

FENGO   Well Matthius, don't just stand there, bring her in.

MATTHIUS drags LILJA in.

Well, well, Matthius. This is a surprise.
How'd yee like to be Fengo's bride, prettygirl?

MATTHIUS   Oh. girl — it's yer lucky day!

LILJA   I thought you gots yerself a bride already, Fengo.
What's wrong wi'the one ye got?

FENGO   What's wrong wi'her, prettygirl? What's wrong wi the wife I gots? I'll tell ye what's wrong with her. She stinks! That's what's wrong wi'her. You don't stink, do ye, prettygirl? Not my prettygirl! Fengo likes you.

MATTHIUS	She dreams about ye, Fengo.
FENGO	Does ye loves yer little Fengo, prettygirl?
MATTHIUS	Course she do, Fengo, course she do.
FENGO	Say somethin sweet to old Fengo. Say somethin all girlie an' sweet. Hey prettygirl? Hey, hey? Something all soft'n girlie'n sweet.

Pause.

LILJA	Bugger yer dog.
FENGO	Matthius, I'm gonna kill you.
MATTHIUS	She do love you Fengo! She do!
FENG.	She'd best say somethin sweet to me, Matthius.
MATTHIUS	She will, honest she will! She's just shy, that's her problem—

MATTHIUS drags her aside.

Girl, come here! I'm countin on you child.
Give Fengo a kiss! Go! Sit on his knee! Now!

He throws her on FENGO's lap. Pause.

FENGO	Well, bonnielass?
LILJA	Well, what?
FENGO	You gonna marrie Fengo like a good little girl?

Pause.

LILJA	Sure I'll marrie you, Fengo.

FENGO	You will?
LILJA	Sure.
FENGO	Well what do ye know?
LILJA	Let's get married today.
MATTHIUS	See, Fengo, see?
FENGO	Whoa! Hold yer horses, prettygirl, hold yer horses! We'll get married, nae ye fear, soon as the Church okays it. Gots to flush out the pottie afore ye shitts in it again, right Matthius?
MATTHIUS	Aye, Fengo, of course.
FENGO	Cah, yer decrepit Matthius. A terrible father too. But this latest gift makes me blind to all yer faults.
MATTHIUS	I'm only serving my friend and Lord.
FENGO	Of course, Matthius. Of course.
MATTHIUS	Is I...still hex-communicated, Fengo?
FENGO	No, Matthius, yer nott. Goodnight my little choke-cherry.
LILJA	Goodnight, my darling Fengo.
MATTHIUS	Move, girl, let's go. Long live Lord Fengo!

Exeunt MATTHIUS and LILJA.

FENGO	The Star of Fengo rises in the North, Now the Fates unveil their gracious plann:

FENGO   (*continued*) A new God, a new and juicy bride;
                  What didd Fengo to deserve such joy?
                  Nae ye mind; the Stars have spake their Will.
                  Fengo rises — and higher shall he still.

                              ***

Scene Seventeenth

MATTHIUS' house.

*LILJA has barred the door. She has a leather bag
and is stuffing things into it. A pounding at the
door. It is MATTHIUS.*

LILJA	What?
MATTHIUS	Open up!
LILJA	In a minute.
MATTHIUS	What are you doing?
LILJA	None of your business—
MATTHIUS	What are you— *(bursting in)* Here...yer packin a bag!
LILJA	I am not.
MATTHIUS	No? What's this about then?
LILJA	I dunno.
MATTHIUS	You dunno, you dunno? Maybe a crack on the snout'll jostle yer memory—

He slaps her in the face.

LILJA	Dadda — Dadda — if you hitt me one more time I will punch you so hard i' the mouth.

MATTHIUS	Oh girl, you'd rue the hour o' yer birth.
LILJA	I already do. Now get out o' my way.
MATTHIUS	Don't you mouth off to yer father, girl—
LILJA	I'll mouth off to my father if I want. I wish you were fukkin DEAD!!
MATTHIUS	WHAT??

He slaps her. She punches him in the mouth.

Why, you—

They fight.

LILJA	You canna hit me no more — I won't let you.
MATTHIUS	Cursed scourge o' my life, what's this bag about then?
LILJA	Mind yer own business.
MATTHIUS	You are my bastard business.
LILJA	I int runnin away, I says!
MATTHIUS	I'll ties you to the post, you little viper!

He cruelly ties her up.

LILJA	Owwwww! Dadda — Dadda, stop and hear! I was goin up the Seacoast, Dad — that's where I was going. To get you some Seashells. Charms for Good Luck! Stop, Dad! I was gonna giv'em ye as a surprise!
MATTHIUS	Girl — if you brought me anything other than grief it would indeed be a surprise.

LILJA	You gots to believe me, Dad — that's the truth.
MATTHIUS	Hah! You wretch! You rotten little liar! Hang you, serpent-tongue! Wrecker of my life!

He gets ready to flog her. She wails.

LILJA	Aaaaaah! No one loves me no matter what I do! No one cares what finally comes of me! I was tryin to be loyall — do somethin good for once! Ohhhh Daddy, Daddy — I want to die...
MATTHIUS	Ohhh stopp it — stopp! Quit curdling at my blood! Don't cry, don't cry lass — it makes my heart hurt.
LILJA	You hate my gutts.
MATTHIUS	I do not hate you.
LILJA	Yer always hitting me and hurting me, Paa.
MATTHIUS	Well, sweetheart, yer always floutin my authority and that hurts me inside too...I try, I try to be a good father to you girl — but, it's hard, it's hard girl...I...I don't know how...
LILJA	Oh beloved Dad. Untie me?
MATTHIUS	Girl, girl you've... You've got your Mother's eyes... I...I never meant to kill her, child — I swear. I — I slappt her with my sword— Oh GODDS!
LILJA	I know, Dad.
MATTHIUS	I'm so ashamed of what I am! Oh godds forgive me...have mercy on old Matthius...

He sobs.

LILJA   It ain't your fault. Nothing is your fault.
                 Yer faultless, Dad. Untie me?

                 Pause. He looks at her. He dries his eyes.

MATTHIUS   You...you still gonna get me some seashells, child?

LILJA   Can I finish packing my bag?

MATTHIUS   You...promise you'll wedd with Fengo, girl?

LILJA   Aye, as ever you say.

                 He unties her.

MATTHIUS   Oh sweetheart. I'll go out and I'll carve you a giant
                 sledd. I'll carve it myself, from solid oak, to last you
                 five hundred lifetimes.

LILJA   Thank you, Dad, staunchmost Dad.

MATTHIUS   I love you Lilja, very much.
                 Goodmorrow then, my sweet child,
                 Goodmorrow, goodmorrow...

                 *He kisses her. He goes. Pause. She is hiding a
                 huge war-axe.*

LILJA   Goodmorrow forever, you doomed son of a bitch.

                             ***

Scene Eighteenth

*The baptism scene. The North Sea. A winter
morning.*

*The whole village is gathering on the beach. The
new dragonhead crosses are erected. HORVENDAL
wears a stolen monk's cowl.*

HORVENDAL   So here's the place: the windy Sealand Shore.
Where one age ends, another does begin.
Old times castoff like weatherbeaten ruggs,
And Denn-mark answers to a Stranger's Godd.
Ohh Powers, if Powers still you be,
Now's the time to manifest your Will:
I'll disguise me in a cowl'd hood,
And finish this, afore the gasping world!
Ssshh! Be silent! Here they do impend.
Watch. And listen. And Justice shall descend.

> *HORVENDAL hoods himself and hides to the
> side. Enter FENGO, GERUTHA, and Vikings.*

FENGO   Heh heh heh. This's been a bigger fuss'n me
weddingfest! Looka me, I'm the force o'wisdom and
progress. Lookit, woman. Lookit Fengo in his
baptismal cloak!

GERUTHA   I can see.

FENGO   Int Fengo a majestic sight?

GERUTHA   Aye, Fengo, aye.

FENGO	They e'en said I could keep this frock. Daft buggers. Here — as soon as I'm done this, I'm gonna hexcommunicate yer sonn — fer slashing me haunches woman! What do you think of that? Hey woman? Hey? Hey?
GERUTHA	I want what you want.
FENGO	You want what Fengo wants? Hah! I hope nott. Else you'd be out shaggin that prettygirl. Hey?
GERUTHA	I—
FENGO	Well, well, the Priests have arriv'd! Lets go! Fengo's afreezin! Do it fast so we can eat.

The priests enter singing. They assemble. The great horn is sounded. Pause.

PETRI	Jesus Christ, oh Holy King of Heaven, God the Father and God the Holy Ghost, We are come to the village of Helsingor To spread Thy Message of Love across the Earth. Amen.
ALL	Amen.
PAAVO	God our Father, thank Ye for Thy Miracles, Thank Ye for the Grace of Thy Son, Jesus Christ. Amen.
ALL	Amen.
FENGO	Do I kneel now?
PAAVO	Aye.
FENGO	In the water?

PAAVO	Aye.
FENGO	Grrrr. Hold me crutches. Make it fast.
PETRI	Christ, Redeemer, let your Light shine over the North Sea; let this Baptism of Fengo the Confessor bring the last of thy children unto Grace. Amen.
FENGO	Couldn't we do this a' home in the friggin bath?
PAAVO	Sshh! Lord Fengo—
FENGO	Just hurry up!
PETRI	Fengo, Lord of Helsingor, kneel before thy Maker, And in His Eyes, confess thy Sinns, That they may be forgiven.
FENGO	Sins? Ye mean the bad things that I done?
PAAVO	Aye, Lord Fengo.
FENGO	Hmmmm, where do I start?

> *HORVENDAL approaches, trembling. FENGO clears his throat disgustingly.*

FENGO	I spake rudely in my time to — well, a lot of people — plus I took things what did not belong to me. Plus I have look'd at wimmen and thought nasty dirty thoughts. These are Fengo's sins and he is so ashamed...
PAAVO	Is that all?
FENGO	Well...I did compare meself to the gods a lot. Plus I swear. And I drink. A whole lot. And that's it.
PAAVO	Nothing else?

FENGO   Well...
I must admit I've slew a lot of folk.
Often for a reason, but just as often not;
Laugh'd at cripples, stole from peasants,
Fornicated like you wouln't believe;
Disembow'l'd Christians, tortur'd helpless animals;
Burn'd down yonder forest to starve the poor;
Betray'd everyone I've met; beat my wife,
Cockwhallop'd every child i' the village,
And said things that int completely true.
Heh heh...
These are my sinns. I am so ashamed.
Oh yeh — plus I smashed me brother's brains.

PAAVO   Let us pray.

FENGO   Aye, let's pray.

            HORVENDAL pounces on FENGO.

HORVENDAL Murderer! Murderer! He said it so hisself!
This bastard int no Christian — he's a murderer!

FENGO   Hey wot?

            HORVENDAL tries to drown him in the sea.

HORVENDAL Murderer! Die you murdering dog!!

            The Vikings pounce on HORVENDAL.

VIKING   Hoy stopp'im!

PAAVO   He's confessed, he's forgiven!

            They pull him off FENGO.

HORVENDAL He ain't sorry — he ain't sorry, he's proud!

FENGO   HE STABBED ME!

PAAVO   Peace, boy, peace! Violence never solved anything!

FENGO   Aye, lad, violence never solved anything!

HORVENDAL   Why, yoouu--

FENGO   Haa haa haa haaaa!!

              Mayhem erupts.

PAAVO   Oh peace, peace, you riotous Danes!
              Have some respect, and from this brawl refrain!

              They subdue him again.

FENGO   I'm forgiven lad, and yer not! Vengeance is not The
              Christian Way!!

HORVENDAL   Dogs ripp your throat, Fengo, I was a Christian
              before you!

FENGO   Well you sure don't look like one now!

PAAVO   Peace!!

HORVENDAL   I'll turn this village against you! I'll rouse the Danish
              Freemen against you!

FENGO   Go ahead and try it — Madd Boy.

              The Vikings laugh. HORVENDAL breaks free.

HORVENDAL   You watch for me Fengo — I'm not what I seem!
              I'll haunt you forever — I'll slay you in your dreams!
              I'm everywhere Fengo — don't dare take a breath!
              Once was I Madd-Boy — but now — am I DEATH!
              I'm everywhere Fengo — I'm EVERYWHERE!!

              He runs out howling. Pause.

PAAVO	I fear that lad might hurt somebody.
FENGO	Aye, I knew he was up to somethin.

>   *GERUTHA has fallen to her knees weeping.*

You! This is all yer fault! I told ye from the
beginning.
A sackful of gold to anyone what captures Young
Horvendal! That goes fer you too, woman. If ye
wants to get baptiz'd, you better move!

>   *She runs out, still in tears.*

Go on! Quit gawkin! Give me my crutches.
Fengo the Confessor has spoken!

>   *The Vikings cheer and run out waving swords.*
>   *FENGO smiles at the priests.*

The Meek rise up; let all of Denn-Mark know,
No man on earth is safe — if Jesus is his Foe.

>   *The priests look at each other sadly.*

***

Scene Ninteenth

The great hall - empty and quiet.

HORVENDAL runs in with his dagger.

HORVENDAL   Mother! Mother! I know you're hiding!
Mother? This is yer Sonn!
Mother? Mother where are you?
Where is that womann? Mother?

    GERUTHA ambushes him from behind.

HORVENDAL   Oh!

GERUTHA   Shut up, boy.

    She holds a dagger to his throat.

Don't fight now — you hear me?

HORVENDAL   Mother, is that you?

GERUTHA   Don't argue wi'me, sonn. Drop yer dagger. Drop it!

    He drops his dagger and she picks it up.

HORVENDAL   Mother, you—

GERUTHA   You said you was a halfwitt.
Now I'm the one what looks a halfwitt.
Bless you, sonn!

    She beats him, drags him by the hair.

HORVENDAL But Momma—

GERUTHA I ain't seen no jott o' peace and quiet,
Not in fortie years o'life upon this earth,
And here I am, I nearly caught my breath—
And you come and stroy'd it, you blisterd seed!

HORVENDAL What're you doin?

GERUTHA What's it look like I'm doin?
I'm gonna slay you, afore they gets the chance.

HORVENDAL Momma, you can't!

GERUTHA No? Watch us and see!
I'll abort you, sonn — as you aborted mee!

>   *She chases him up the wall. He climbs into the*
>   *rafters.*

HORVENDAL Momma — it's Horvendal — yer sweet and precious
sonn!
How can you turn upon me in my darkest hour?
Remember the way I used to cry and cry,
You rock'd me in me cradle, sang me songs...
Momma — hear me! What times we used to have!
Listen: listen Momma: don't you remember?

GERUTHA No!

>   *He sings an ancient lullaby.*

HORVENDAL Sleep child, oh sweet child, oh ember of my soul...
The four winds protect thee, oh ember of my soul...

GERUTHA Stop. No! No! I hear you nott.
Noooo! My babie, my babie's dead!

*He sings it again. She staggers back. Suddenly
she drops the dagger, falls to her knees, sobbing
wretchedly. Pause.*

HORVENDAL   Mother? Mother? Aye Maa, it's me.
Look ye my visage — yer sonn's here — look see.

She looks up. Pause.

GERUTHA   Oh Sonn, Sonn. You were such a bonnie babie boy...
How come ye grew to be so horrible?

HORVENDAL   Momma, I int so horrible —
I'll be yer tiny one again...
Cast aside the bitterness between us;
Danish Skies at long last shall be blue!
I'll build for you a house of finest cedar,
There you'll live, in blissful blissful rest!
Think of it Momma, a end to Toil and Woe!
Believe me Momma! The Truth, yer Heart doth
know!

He inches down to her. She sobs.

GERUTHA   Ohh child, I don't deserve no kindness.
Ohh what a wretched life I've lived...
I loves you sonn, I always wept for you;
I ne'er could tell it ye...but I do...

He holds her and they both cry.

HORVENDAL   There there Momma, you never meant no wrong;
Against the blast of fortune, a mother's love is strong.
Whatever else were perish'd, I knew me Maa weren't dead.
Help us then help us! Lets crush that Fengo's head!

GERUTHA   WHAT? What say you? Yooouu devious Maggot!
Thought you could worm away my batter'd heart?
Pah! You wolfpupp! You sneagling scorpion!
Viprous mann-snake! Here's what I think of you!

She comes at him with the daggers.

HORVENDAL Momma, Momma, yer housin up with Evil—

GERUTHA Shut up, sonn, yer evil too.

HORVENDAL Momma, Momma — Fengo slew my Paa!

GERUTHA SO WHAT?? Ye thinks he dint deserve it?
Fengo's a bunnyrabbit next to yer Paa!

HORVENDAL Calm yerself Momma — put down yer daggers! Drop
them! Help me Godds!

He seizes her by the wrists.

GERUTHA Someone! Someone!

HORVENDAL Drop them I sez—

GERUTHA Help us anyone! Fengo!

HORVENDAL Stop it!

GERUTHA Matthius! He were right to wanna see you strung—
Matthius! He spotted you, right from the start—
Matthius! Brethrens! Someone! Anyone!
They'll fix you. Help Help!!

*Pause. Enter LILJA, covered in blood. Smiling,
holding something behind her back.*

GERUTHA Child?

HORVENDAL Lilja?

GERUTHA What are you doing?

LILJA Madd Boy. Angel. Look what I done.

She holds up her father's head.

HORVENDAL   Gods have mercy!

LILJA   Haill, Fatherslayer!
Bless me, Saint Horvendal. I slew my father too.

HORVENDAL   Slew yer father, girl? What moved you to this?
They'll ripp you apart, girl!

LILJA   I love you, Madd Boy.

HORVENDAL   Oh Momma—

GERUTHA   Don't either of you move.
You ain't no children noways — you're BEASTS!

HORVENDAL   Momma—

GERUTHA   Nay, I heed you nott!
Twill joy me joy me to see ye both hung!
Die!!

> *HORVENDAL grabs LILJA's dagger. There is a struggle, mother against son. Then GERUTHA falls back, the knife in her side.*

HORVENDAL   Momma?

GERUTHA   Ow, ow...

HORVENDAL   Maa, I never—

GERUTHA   Don't speak to me!

HORVENDAL   You made me do it, twas yer own fault.
You know it was. Are you alright?

GERUTHA   Piss off.

HORVENDAL	I swear, Maa!
GERUTHA	Runn — let me bleed. What do I matter? Do as e'er ye need.

Vikings shout offstage.

HORVENDAL	Oh you torture-godds, all its turn'd awrong! Oh Warr unwinnable, hopeless all along! Fengo he lives, Fengo's turn'd a Christian, Me mother's stabb'd, the girl's lost her mind— And mee, Mother, Mother what am I? A Dead Man! Runn, girl. To Oblivion we go.
LILJA	Is that near Jerusalem?
HORVENDAL	Aye, somethere thereabouts.

He throws his mother a rag.

	Here Momma, clean yerself up. I'm real sorry, I am, I am.
GERUTHA	Get lost!
HORVENDAL	(*to LILJA*) Oh, girl, girl, girl.

He runs out. LILJA follows. FENGO bursts in with the Vikings and monks.

FENGO	Cah, woman, can't you do anything? Adds thatt to yer list of botch-ups! (*seeing MATTHIUS' head*) Matthius! Hoy! What happened to you? See Holy-ladds? See what goes on up here? Don't just stand there! After him, after him! Come on wifie, look alive!

FENGO and VIKINGS and MONKS exit.
GERUTHA is left alone.

GERUTHA   Farewell, you cancer of the womb,
May you swiftly meet your doom;
Poor old Mother's left to face
The consequence of her disgrace;
Menn like you are free to die,
And suffer not the lott of I;
Poor old Mother's trapped on earth;
What a joy — the gift of birth!

A bleeding GERUTHA crawls off alone.

***

Twentieth Scene

RAGNAR's return. Soon after. The same place.

He stands looking at the ransacked house. He sees his father's head. Pause.

RAGNAR   What in fuck's been going on here?
I buggers off fer two weeks and comes back to this!
FENGO, you cudgeon, you cankerous sledmutt,
What's been goin on here while Ragnar was a-whalin?
FENGO!

Enter FENGO and the Vikings.

FENGO   Ragnar lad!

RAGNAR   Who slew my father, Fengo?

FENGO   How was yer whalin trip?

RAGNAR.   I'll give you a whalin trip, Fengo!

FENGO   Easy, boy, easy! Remember I'm yer Lord!

RAGNAR   You ain't no bloody lord if you dont do yer bloody
jobb! Who chopp'd off me Dadda's head? Where's me
sister? Spit it out, Fengo, you crocodile, what have
you done with my sister?

FENGO   Fengo int done nothin so you put yer sword away.
It's Horvendal, the so-call'd Madd-Boy. He's the one
what done this.

RAGNAR	Horvendal? Horvendal?
FENGO	Aye, him and yer sister — who it turns out is nowt but a whoore!
RAGNAR	I'll murder him!
FENGO	They was dancin, Ragnar, on yer dead Father's corpse, Singin, Ragnar's a pixieboy, Ragnar's a pixie! Then the two o' them friggerd off into the sunset, Probly acopulatin as we speak!
RAGNAR.	Enough! Enough! I'll hack out his liver! I'll wind his steamin gutts round a tree! Which way did he go Fengo? Whence did they frigger? Whence did they haulaway? Speak!
FENGO	Easy ladd easy, this here's a Christian land. We gots to take the Boy, legally. Administer the punishment, slowly and deliberately. This here's the Christian Way.
RAGNAR.	The Christian Way?
FENGO	Aye, it's a New Age, innit? To everythin there be a season, To every season a meaning.
RAGNAR	What?
FENGO	A time for warr, ladd, and a time fer hate. A time for fightin, and a time fer dying; A time for combatt, a time for wrangling, A time for torture, a time for hackin out spleens—
RAGNAR	I'm gonna murder him!
FENGO	No you ain't! Yer gonna haul the boy home to Fengo! Fengo will dispense Godd's Justice, Godd's way. Do you believe in Godd boy? Say yes.

RAGNAR   Aye.

FENGO   Good lad. Kneel down o' the ground.
         I gots to baptise ye i' the new faith. Kneel down.

RAGNAR   Why?

FENGO   Just do it boy!

RAGNAR   Yer a pain i' the arse, Fengo.

FENGO   Shh.

FENGO pours holy water on his head.

RAGNAR   Hey!

FENGO   The Lord is my shepherd what I don't want,
         He maketh me lie down in green water.
         He deploreth my soul, my cupp runneth over,
         For we walk in the shadow of death forever, Amen.

RAGNAR   What the fuck was that?

FENGO   I just made you a Christian Soldier. Whatever ye do,
         from here on in, ye do on behalf of the Lord Jesus
         Christ, understand?

RAGNAR   Lord who?

FENGO   The fella I been talkin about!

RAGNAR   Oh yeh, yeh right.

FENGO   Round up every able-bodied man.

RAGNAR   Aye, Fengo.

FENGO   Build yerself a Christian Horde.

RAGNAR   Aye, Fengo, aye.

FENGO   Comb yee this icy wilderness. Bring this boy to Fengo.
But don't ye forget kid, I want the boy — alive.

RAGNAR   I'll bring him home to you, Fengo — I swear to you,
right now. In the name of Skull-Byter, Sword of me
Granpapaa, I swear I'll deliver this boy to you.

FENGO   Go, Brave Ragnar, go i' the name o' Christ,
Go forth and let Jesus guide yer Sword!

RAGNAR   Did ye hear that, Skull-Byter? We gots a jobb to do!
Heighyupp, Skull-Byter! Long Live Lord Fengo!

RAGNAR runs out bellowing.

FENGO   Ah youth, the promise o'the future.
What a joy to see events unfold.

GERUTHA is still sitting there, bleeding.

Stop sittin around here like a bump on a logg.
Get yer stupid cloak on. Go seek out the Madd Boy.

He leaves. Drums sound. Vikings roar.
GERUTHA crawls off the stage.

***

Scene Twenty-First

Bitter wind. Midnight. Wolves howl.
HORVENDAL and LILJA are in the icy
fens.They huddle inside HORVENDAL's cloak.

HORVENDAL   Stop jumpin up and down, girl, yer wastin body heat.

LILJA   I'm cold.

HORVENDAL   Well huddle up.

LILJA   I thought you said Jerusalem was a hot country.

HORVENDAL   Well this ain't Jerusalem, is it? This is the Fenns. Where Grendel and his Mother lived. Gods' Death, it's afreezin! Look ye around, girl. Make sure there int no Gods comin. I don't wanna see no Gods. They're makin me confus'd. (*long pause*) Lilja?

LILJA   Aye?

HORVENDAL   Girl, are you alright?

LILJA   Aye, love, thank ye, love, I'm turn'd to a beautiful swann.

HORVENDAL   But think what you done, girl, and with your Christ awatchin!

LILJA   Ohhh bleed me again, sweet saint, I done it acause Christ was watchin.

She kisses him all over. He struggles free.

HORVENDAL   Come on, girl, ease up — let's build a fire. Gather up
some kindling afore we perish.

LILJA   I'll follow you to the ends of the earth, Saint
Horvendal.

HORVENDAL   Oh girl.

LILJA   Me, I seen the light thru you.
You an' me we're gonna rid the world of Evil.
You an' me we're gonna purify the Earth.
You an' me we're gonna massacre the Devil!
Ain't we, Saint Horvendal, ain't we?

HORVENDAL   No, girl, we ain't.

LILJA   What? What say you? What mean ye we ain't?
Saint Horvendal? Love? What do you mean?

HORVENDAL   Oh sweet soul, I should've heeded when you beckond,
And run away afore this all began;
I'd be sittin, sleepin in a Palm-Tree now:
Not waitin to be eaten up by Wolves!
Sweet lost soul; ne'er ask'd you for this World!
Ne'er asked yee be cast in fray with me;
What Godd, what blind and mighty Power,
Could create both Crocodiles — and thee?

LILJA   What're you telling me?

HORVENDAL   Too much blood's been spilt. Way too much.
Somewhere, someways, the circle has to end.
More than this, girl, my arms and legs've hadd it.
I'm sick. I'm tired. I'm brokendown. I quit.

Pause. She rises.

LILJA   Get yee upp.

HORVENDAL   What?

LILJA   On your FEET! We've a Holy War to wage!
             I int quittin ever, EVER — till every Vikingman is
             dead!

HORVENDAL   Girl, stopp it—

LILJA   No, I'll stop it NOTT! Dint ye hear Lord Jesus
             ahowlin when ye plunged yer sword in Lord Fengo?
             Weren't he ahowlin and adancin and festivitatin with
             Joy?

                  Pause.

HORVENDAL   Girl, I nee slay'd him.

LILJA   WHAT??

HORVENDAL   I nee slayd him. He got away.

LILJA   Fengo got away? You let Fengo get away?
             You let Fengo, clobberer, cockswipe — GET AWAY?

HORVENDAL   Forget it, girl, — it's done.

LILJA   You said you slay'd him — you said you putt him
             i'the ground—you said you whippd him, wiped him
             from the surface of Godds Earth!

HORVENDAL   I said no such thing! Calm yerself down.
             The nightmare is over, girl. Let's eat.

                  Pause.

LILJA   We're turnin back.

HORVENDAL   What?

LILJA   I said, we're turnin back! We're turnin around to do
                what you said you'd do but didn't, you lying
                floundering SLAVE!!

HORVENDAL   No we ain't!

                She explodes, punching, kicking him.

LILJA   Coward! Coward! You lying Christless Coward!
                You deceiv'd — you LIED to prettygirl!
                Yooouu stoat! You pus-leech! You worthless wastrel!
                You cyst-ridden changeling from a dogg's arse!
                Oh, SLAVE!

HORVENDAL   Girl, yer mouth — yer the one said runn away!

LILJA   Well yer the one swore he would slay Fengo!

HORVENDAL   Well, girl, I gone and chang'd me mind!

LILJA   You chang'd yer mind one too many times! I'm makin
                decisions now, Mad Boy, and I say we turn back!

HORVENDAL   No! No! I smell a foul conclusion!
                Please, girl, don't go!

LILJA   Unhand me child, I'll do yer jobb for ye.
                What mov'd me to put my faith in you?
                Ha! Madd Boy! Sadd Boy more like.
                Give up yer sword Sadd Boy — now!

                HORVENDAL grabs the blade and slices his hand.

HORVENDAL   Owww!

LILJA   Ha. Serves ye right.
                Here — give up yer wooly cloakings too.
                A Mann's job requires mannly garb,
                As well as a Mann to fit them.
                You — can wear my dress!

HORVENDAL   Hey!

She pulls off his hooded cloak, throws him her mantle.

LILJA   There. Lookit ye. Pretty little Sadd Boy.
From this time henceforth — Lilja shall be you!
Go on Sadd Boy. Get ye to Jerusalem.
Go tell Jesus why yer dressed like a girl!

HORVENDAL   Wait, girl!

LILJA   What, girl?

HORVENDAL   Thou Shalt Not Kill!
Berserkery is not a strategy enough!

LILJA   Stay you here. You gave me nowt but pain;
The Destinie of Worlds is built with Gutts, not Brains.
A wretch like you, tis best had died at birth,
Than wasted precious Time upon this Earth!

HORVENDAL   But, girl, girl—

LILJA   No words, no more!

HORVENDAL   Girl, don't leave me—

LILJA   VENGEANCE!

She runs into the night. Wind and wolf-crie rise.

HORVENDAL   Oh no...

***

Scene Twenty-Second

The forest at night. Very dark.

Enter RAGNAR with Vikings. They catch their breath.

RAGNAR
No relentin, fellas, no relentin.
Moon or Sunn, we're bound to do this task.

VIKING
Haill!

RAGNAR
Tells ye what, me boys, tells ye what,
Split we up and comb this icy Fenn.

VIKINGS
Haill! Haill Ragnar! Haill!

RAGNAR
Wait!

RAGNAR speaks to his sword.

What's the matter Skull-Byter, old boy?
Ye smell sommet? Ragnar smell sommet too.
Lie low everybody lie low! Shh!!
Ohh stealth! Oh ambush! Here the Madd Boy comes!

They all hide in the bushes. Enter LILJA as THE MAD BOY, disguised in a cloak.

LILJA
Who's there? Who's that in there?
A skulking Viking. I aspose ye skulks fer mee.
Hello Plundermann. I can see yer helmet there!
Come on out the bunch o'yez,
Bring yer hellbound corses i'the light.

They emerge.

RAGNAR   Well, well, well, if it int the Madd Boy.

LILJA   Well, well, well, if it int the Dead Boys.

RAGNAR   Wha'tve you done wi' the girl, Madd Boy?

LILJA   Nothin youz ain't done already.
Come on — haul forth — rush me all at once.
Madd Boy's out to de-worm Dennmark!

They surround her.

ALL   Ho ho! Brave notion! Oh Notion! Oh Brave!

LILJA   Try and stop me, you lumbering slaves!

RAGNAR   *(drawing his sword)* Behold yee Skull-Byter.

LILJA   Skull-Byter? Arse-Byter more like!

RAGNAR   Ohh laddie when I'm adone wi' you,
There'll be nothin left o' you to burn.

LILJA   Oh laddie when I'm adone with you,
Oh you'll hang screamin on the gates of Hell.

RAGNAR   Foolish Mad Boy!

LILJA   Damn'd Dead Boy!

RAGNAR   Prepare to die, Mad Boy!

LILJA   Prepare yee to kiss the Devil's Arse!

RAGNAR   HAA!

RAGNAR swings and knocks the sword from her hands.

Hey? What was you sayin?

*They both lunge for the sword. RAGNAR gets it
and turns on LILJA with two swords.*

What was you sayin Mad Boy to mee?
Disgrace yee my Familie? Disgrace yee my Sword?
Hey Madd Boy? Hey? Who's a Madd Boy now?

LILJA   *Liljaaa!!*

RAGNAR   Axe-menn, axe-menn, let yer axes fall!
Shut up the Madd Boy once and for all!
Don't lettim get away boys — chop him! chop him!

*They all descend on her with swords and axes.
Blackout. A horrible scream.*

***

Scene Twenty-Third

The next morning. The house of FENGO.

FENGO Ahhh the morrow. The Christian Sunn's arised.
Another morn, a Golden Day is come;
Fengo's Day, the first of many pending,
What Good Deed shall Fengo render first?

GERUTHA Water, Fengo.

FENGO Nae chance, mother.

GERUTHA I don't feel so good.

FENGO You don't feel so good?
Think how Fengo feels, seein yer gloomie face!
Go on! Quit bothrin me! Yer exploitin Fengo's
charitie.

A loud wailing offstage.

What the hell is that..?

Another wail.

Sounds like bully Ragnar.

*Enter RAGNAR, weeping desperately, carrying a
bloody bundle.*

RAGNAR Fengo!! Fengo!!

FENGO What's the matter with you?

RAGNAR	Fengo — Fengo...

He drops LILJA's mangled corpse.

FENGO	What have you got there?
RAGNAR	Lilja, oh Liljaaa, oh sweet, ooh innocent child—
FENGO	What you do to her. Ragnar?
RAGNAR	I int done nothin! You can't pin nothin on me! Madd Boy, he done this! I found her like that! Oh girl, oh say something sister! Oh Skull-Byter — why didn't you tell me?

FENGO prods her remains.

FENGO	She don't look very talkative.
RAGNAR	Madd Boy, he done that.
FENGO	Of course, me boy — you said.
RAGNAR	It's true, Fengo, I dint do nothin! I barely murder'd her at all! Ohhh sister sister sister sister sister...that Madd Boy destroy'd everythin I ever lov'd...!

He sobs convulsively.

FENGO	Boy, stop, ye needn't say aught else. Axemen get this girl out of here.
GERUTHA	I wish that was me.

They drag the body out.

FENGO	Hie thee up lad. Heft yer howlings inn. Swabb that childish snooling from yer nose: Suck yer pain back! Hold it in yer gutts! Let it burn — and fuel ye for the chase!

FENGO	(*continued*) Quit yer blubberin. She int our prioritie. Where's the Mad Boy? He's still on the loose!
RAGNAR	What sort of bastard'd chops up a little girl? Promise Fengo, you'll hang him on a tree!
FENGO	Of course, boy.
RAGNAR	With a sign on his neck, sayin 'I chops up little girls! She were my sister Fengo my little babie sister — oooohhhHHHHH VENGEANCE!!-
FENGO	Alright, ladd — look, ye can slay him. But it has to seem a haccident, you hear? Mulch him up and scrunch him up and down. Make it look like the wolves done it.
RAGNAR	Oh thank you, Fengo, thank you, thank you—
FENGO	Aye, son.
RAGNAR	Fengo, I swear o'me grave I nee done touch'd her! I int no badmann Fengo, I int no lass-killer—
FENGO	Course ye int, stoutie, yer a Christian Warrior. Now go.
RAGNAR	Oh thank you, Fengo. Men we're goin back ouside! Cmon Menn, we're allowed to kill the Madd Boy!
ALL	Hurrrahh!
RAGNAR	VENGEAAAANCE!!

He storms out, followed by Vikings. Elsewhere, GERUTHA cradles the dead LILJA. She sings her lullaby.

***

Scene Twenty-Fourth

*A frozen swamp. Darkest night. Wolves run
through the trees. The skeleton of a cannibalized
wolf is left as they scatter. Enter HORVENDAL,
delerious, wearing nothing but his breeches.*

HORVENDAL Where did I go wrong, fates? Where did I go wrong?
Were it the time I stood by and forgave me Uncle
Fengo? Or the time I come to dream of this Revenge?
Were it the time I came to faith in Jesus, or the time I
cast him off? Or was it all those times wrong? Were it
me birth what was wrong? Is anybody out there
alistenin to Horvendal? Hello? Or is the heavens dark,
deserted; as empty as Fengo's Eyehole? Aye, it's his
Eye-hole, come to gulf me upp! Yawning, swirling,
topless, bottomless! Help! Hello? What's here?

He trips over the wolf-skull then lifts it up.

I nae knew yee. I can guess ye well.
Where yer doggish soul went, there should Horvendal.
Howso died ye, sure it served you right,
And so I plummet howling, into that good night...

He chops a hole in the ice with the skull.

Go dead doggie! Show us the way!
Lead this Blind Boy into the Afterworld!

He howls, plunges into the hole in the ice.

***

Scene Twenty-Fifth

The hall at Helsingor.

GERUTHA crawls behind BROTHER PAAVO.
She is in a terrible state.

GERUTHA   Brother Paavo. Brother Paavo.

PAAVO   Aye, what is it?

GERUTHA   I wants to ask you—

PAAVO   Make it quick.

GERUTHA   Is it true Brother Paavo — is it true what it says —
Jesus he lov'd even the wretchedest and lowest, the
saddest, most brokedown souls on Earth?

PAAVO   Aye.

GERUTHA   Do ye think he'd a loved me too?

PAAVO   Perhaps.

GERUTHA   Ohhh if only he could! Baptise me, Brother Paavo,
baptise me afore I dies...

PAAVO   Nae, madam, I cannot.

GERUTHA   What?

PAAVO   Fengo said I int to baptize yee.

GERUTHA	Not to baptize me? How am I to get to Heaven?
PAAVO	Fengo said he don't want ye there.
GERUTHA	Not to get to Heaven? Brother, I begs yer mercy! Take mercy on a repentant, dying woman!
PAAVO	Sorry, madam. His whims I must permit. Your Husband is God's Gateway to the Danes. Without his might, our influence is naught. For the greater good, madam. Forgive me.

> *Enter FENGO, with Vikings and BROTHER PETRI.*

Morning, Lord Fengo.

FENGO	What's goin on in here? Didn't I tells you not to talk to the Bretherens?
GERUTHA	But—
FENGO	Didn't I tells you, woman — not to talk to the Bretherens? Oh wife of mine! This Betrayall o'yers cuts deep! I'm astartin to doubts yer Loyaltie!
GERUTHA	But I'm dyin, Fengo! I'm dyin—
FENGO	Aye, woman, so you said.
GERUTHA	Fengo — curse you. Look upon these eyes. You've slain me! I — HATE you Fengo!!
FENGO	Aaah! She hates me. Now the Truth comes out: Now you see the source of Fengo's grief! Hie thee hence, Old Mortality; float away you old stool, Hasten yer demise —aquitt ye this realm. This hand — will hoist youz up no more.

Pause.

GERUTHA   Yooou'll suffer for this, Fengo, I know you will.
               I don't know how, and I don't know when,
               But I do know — it will be slooow, and bloody;
               All the torture, all the grief what you've inflicted
               Will come back upon you, Fengo, ohhh it shall!
               An' I'll be laughin — my ghost will be laughin,
               As you choke up bloody clumps of gore;
               So die I, Fengo — free from out this hole.
               At least in Hell —there's someone wants my soul...

               She dies. FENGO watches her. Pause.

FENGO   That woman broke my heart.

PAAVO   She didn't mean it, Fengo, she were hysterical.

FENGO   I gave my life to her.

PAAVO   Peace good lord, leadership's a hard lot.

FENGO   Alas, good brother, sometimes so it seems.
               Perhaps true Loyaltie — comes only but in dreams...

               Dead LILJA sings.

                              ***

Scene Twenty-Sixth

The fens. Wolves howl.

HORVENDAL emerges from a frozen river, still alive.

HORVENDAL   Useless useless — can't even drown meself.
Me gutts are e'en more guttless than me brains!
Where am I now? Further down the river.
It's washed me back, cross all the land I gain'd.

     A howl.

Aye Wolvens, howl, howl!
Tear apart young Horvendal the fool!
Carry me off unto yer Wolfish Lair,
And do whate'er it is ye Were-wolves do.
Oh Death, tranquility, haul me off to sleep.
Come on, come on, I'm tryin to freeze to death!

     A voice on the wind.

VOICE   Hoorvendaaal, Hoorvendaaal....

HORVENDAL   Piss off! You bugger'd with my head!
Heyoff, Father, I heed you nott!
Go venge your bloodie self!

VOICE   Hooorvendaaaal....Hooorvendaaaal...

HORVENDAL   No! No! I'll drive you hence!
Come on out you Wormbound Warlord!
I'll crush your howling head!

A rising light.

HORVENDAL   What's this? Who's this? No! Not a Wolvish Spirit!
No...No it can't be...
Where in hell were you?

> *Out of the trees comes a bloody, ragged little
> man. He wears a crown of thorns and a loincloth.
> It is JESUS. The real JESUS. He cries tears of
> blood.*

CHRIST   Madd Boy, Horvendal; to you the Christ must turn;
Behold your cast-out Saviour; Mankind will never
learn.

HORVENDAL   What??

CHRIST   Ohh Horvendal: my shining shatterd Angell.
How you failed me! Failed my Path of Love.
Ohh my Hope-Child, how I tried to reach you!
All is soiled now. Listen to your Christ:

Turn Ye Back — Save my Strangled Gospel.
Turn Ye Back — Go Mend the Harm they've done.
Slay thine Uncle! Go take thy Viking Vengeance!
Stop him! Stop him! Oh Poisoned Love-Truth!
Turn Back- and Slay that Mann!

> *He raises his arms. His wrists are pierced.*

HORVENDAL   But your book says—

CHRIST   All is soiled, Horvendal! Viking, go home.
Do as your savage heart bids you.

HORVENDAL   Forgive me Jesus.

CHRIST   I wait for you...

HORVENDAL   Forgive me!

> *JESUS vanishes into the snow. Pause.*
> *HORVENDAL turns and faces north.*

HORVENDAL Ohh Redemption. Redemption in the Night!
Ohh Shining Hope, you've found us!
We'll set these Fates aright!

Liljaa!

> *He staggers back home.*

***

Scene Twenty-Seventh

An empty place by the sea. Early morning.

The two old sisters are weaving a shroud. ANNA has a pot of boiled seaweed.

INGA   Mornin, sister.

ANNA   Aye, mornin.

INGA   How be you today?

ANNA   Gotta splittin headache, don't I? Here, it may be my imaginin, but I'll swear when Fengo baptised me, he delibrately pull'd my hair and shook me up and down.

INGA   Well that's his way, innit? He loves his people, but it's a tough sort of love.

ANNA   Aye but when I come up choking, he laughed a'me! That's not very nice. Thank Jesus I int in his family.

INGA   Oh well, it ain't for us to question. Let's just sit back and complain and let our leaders destroy us.

ANNA   Aye it's prob'ly all for the best.

INGA   Aye.

ANNA   Here, what think ye of all this God and Jesus and Thundergod stuff? Think ye it's true?

INGA   Ohh, of course not. Lies and superstition. Everybody
              knows the world's rul'd by Elves.

              Behind them staggers a ranting HORVENDAL.

              Here, what's that? Comin over the hill!

ANNA   Not another Ghost! Wait! It's the Madd Boy!

INGA   Horvendal! It's the Young Horvendal!
              Hoy ahoy! Good morrow, Madd Boy!

              HORVENDAL stops and looks at them.

HORVENDAL   I int no Coward!!

ANNA   What did he say?

INGA   He said I int no Coward.

HORVENDAL   Fengo—

INGA   And we int Fengo. We're two old wimmen.
              He thinks we're Fengo!

ANNA   You silly Madd Boy.

HORVENDAL   Liljaaa... Liljaaaa... Forgive me Lilja...
              Oh Liljaa....oh help—

              He collapses.

INGA   Well he's in a bad state.

ANNA   Aye what do we do?

INGA   Help him.

ANNA   Help him? But he's a enemie o' the people!

INGA   Enemy nothin. Look at the boy.

> *INGA feeds him.*

> Just think, sister, just think. To be cast out. To be a fugitive from the Law. To starve and suffer and perish. All for astrivlin with his fates.

ANNA   What a twitt.

INGA   Still.

> *THE MAD BOY stirs.*

HORVENDAL   Liljaaa — where is the girl, Lilja?

INGA   He speaks!

HORVENDAL   You! Old wimmen! Where is the girl, Lilja?

ANNA   Who?

INGA   The odd girl? The wee funnie one?

ANNA   Funny you should ask. Sister and me we be weavin her shroud.

HORVENDAL   Shroud? Shroud?

ANNA   Aye, fer windin her up in! Cremation's tomorrow.

INGA   She's died you see.

HORVENDAL   Died? But how?

ANNA   Strook by a meteor. Int that what they said?

HORVENDAL   AAAAHHHH!! DIED!! And Fengo lives! Oh spite! I shine, I rise, girl — give us that Shroud!

INGA   Hoy!

HORVENDAL   Biddies, give us that Shroud—

                He grabs the shroud.

                Good wimmen assist me, I'll tell you what to do!

INGA   Oh leave us out o' this, sonn. We're sick and feeble.

ANNA   Aye, yer a big strong Mad Boy. You can murder
Fengo by yerself.

HORVENDAL   Wimmen, I beggs ye—

INGA   Leave off of us, Mad Boy!

ANNA   Here — don't be handlin my sister! Hoy!!

INGA   Now go on — go on — or I'll hitt ye with this kelp!
We don't like ye no more. Nasty Mad Boy.

ANNA   Aye.

                They drive him away.

HORVENDAL   When you and you and you and you are dead,
Who is it they'll remember? ME!
A Plague upon you lazie fatted stumps
What sitt and pick yer blisters and complain!
Who ist what fought for you? Who struggl'd for yer
sinns?
Whose Tale will thunder, glorious, forever,
In lands unheard of, in glory-times to come?-
ME! The Madd Boy. Horvendal — that's who!
You watch me world, watch me! I done this all for
you!
SALVATION!!

He staggers off. The old wimmen look at each other.

ANNA   Hmm.

INGA   Anyway...

They go back to work.

***

Scene Twenty-The-Eighth

FENGO's hall.

FENGO is drinking with the monks and Vikings.

FENGO Hah haaaaa!! Dint the ol' girl flare up? Didn't she flare up like a blob o' fish-oil? Burn'd fer hours she. Brighter than a torch! 'Spect its all the lard an' blubber like, hey? All them pancakes she ett in her stupid life! Hey, Brother Paavo, hey?

PAAVO She was your wife.

FENGO Ahhh, I'll get over it. I'll get me a new one. Besides, it int Fengo's way to be sadd. Drink up! Tomorrow we burn the little girl. Old whatisnames' girl. Haa, ye shoulda seen her knucklehead brother when he dragg'd her carcass home. Howl'd like a babby. What a twit. Cheers lads — to the clergy!

ALL To the clergy! To the clergy!

FENGO Here, Brother Paavo, watch us drink ale thru our nose.

Enter RAGNAR, exhausted, tears in his eyes.

RAGNAR Fengo!

FENGO Ragnar, what are you doing here?

RAGNAR I can't find the bugger.

FENGO	Well I said don't come back till you did!
RAGNAR	A man's gotta sleep.
FENGO	A man's gotta sleep. Listen to the boy, Brother Paavo.
PAAVO	You pixie!
FENGO	See, laddie, the Church condemns ye! You go right back outside and fetch the Mad Boy!

FENGO and the monks laugh.

RAGNAR	You...DOGG, Fengo! You gutstuffin curr!
FENGO	What did you say?
RAGNAR	You int done nothin, Fengo, to help me in this task!
FENGO	I have too.
RAGNAR	You have NOTT! You been sittin on yer lazie arse stuffin yer face! I done everything! I been huntin him fer days! He int nowhere I tells you! Nowhere!
FENGO	Well you don't look good enough.
RAGNAR	You just sit there all smarlyfaced sayin "Jesus Christ did this, Jesus Christ did that." You ain't no leader, yer a slobb!
FENGO	Say that again?
RAGNAR	Look at you, you fat pig! Ere, you got food in yer beard! Leaders is suppos'd to be inspirin. Yer fuckin disgustin, Fengo!
FENGO	What did you say? (*rising*) Are you challengin Fengo in front of these Holy Brothers?

RAGNAR   I'm sayin—

FENGO   I'm sayin, do as yer told. Remember who I am,
           laddie, cripple or not. You want inspirin, I'll inspire
           you with this! (*swinging his crutch at him*) Now piss
           off — we're havin a theological conference. Go on, I
           say! Lagabout boy. Thank God he's got his father's
           brains! Ha!

           RAGNAR leaves.

FENGO   You — Songman. Writes us a song.

VIKING   Aye, Lord Fengo.

FENGO   Writes us a song — the Tale of Lord Fengo!
           Speak of the Madd Boy, and his floundering
           misdeeds!!
           Comb ye the northland, let it ring through every
           village!
           Heyupp! Up yer bumms axe-menn! We're goin to a
           Funerall!

           Drums. Cheers. Scene change. The Viking sings:

VIKING   Wealth must die, and Kindred die,
           A Man himself must likewise die,
           But Fame and Glory never die,
           For him who achieves it well;
           Goats must die, and Kindred die,
           A Mann himself must likewise die,
           But one thing is shall never die,
           The Verdict on each Man who dies...

                        ***

Scene Twenty-Ninth

The conclusion: Morning. Music: "Dies Irae"
The dragonhead crosses are erected. The north
coast. A great funeral pyre.

Enter the monks, Vikings, and villagers with
torches. A shrouded corpse is carried in, bound on
a bier. FENGO wears pious gear. The body is
tossed on the pyre.

FENGO
Hold off yer torches just a little while;
Gots to allow for any tardie guests.
Let's remember this girl, the example that she set.
A good and gentle angel, inspirin to us all...
At times like this, we often do reflect,
Does life, does death, harbour any hope?
Or is we haccidents, toss'd upon this earth,
Doomed to fight and hack each others bones?
I tell ye verily, look upon this girl,
And try to say to mee, there's no hope for this world.

PAAVO
Amen.

FENGO
Courageous men of Denn-mark:
An elemental battle is risin on our shores!
The Winds of Barbarism howl to engulf us.
Thursday mornin marks a new momentous Year;
The One Thousanth Annum of Our Lord Jesus
Christ...
Will Denn-Mark stand for Crueltie or Mercie?
Is we Animals or is we Christian Menn?
See ye Godd! A change upon us now is come,
And all the World will soon know who we be!

ALL	Amen.
FENGO	But enough of me, what more ist can be said? My humble words can never heal this loss. All a man can say is — Godd is Love; Let's torch this child, and praise the Lord above.
ALL	Amen.
RAGNAR	Hang on a sec afore ye burns her. Ragnar wants to speak some parting words.
FENGO	Dammit boy we done wrapt her up.
RAGNAR	Shut up, Fengo — she's my sister and I'm gonna say my bit!
FENGO	Grrrr. Hurry up.

RAGNAR holds up his sword.

RAGNAR	I, Ragnar, sonn of dead Matthius, Do here give up Skull-Byter, sword o' me Gran-papaa. Lie thou, Skull-Byter, keep this girl from harm, Ragnar the Brave — shall ne'er again bear arms.
FENGO	What are ye doing?
RAGNAR	Farewell, sister. Fare thee well, Skull-Byter. May all fighting men heed my example.
FENGO	Oh fuck, not another one.
RAGNAR	What's this?

HORVENDAL is inside LILJA's shroud. He seizes the sword.

HORVENDAL	Haaaa!!

RAGNAR   Madd Boy!!

FENGO   Horvendal!!

> *HORVENDAL leaps out and impales RAGNAR on Skull-Byter.*

HORVENDAL   Die, bullyboy!

PAAVO   Fly bretheren!

HORVENDAL   And this is for you, and this is for you, and this is for you too!! (*stabbing RAGNAR*) Had enough?

RAGNAR   Bless you Mad Boy...thou hast served me well...

> *He dies. HORVENDAL turns on the crowd.*

HORVENDAL   Stand still! Don't any of ye move.
            Madd Boy's come to claim his Shining Fate:
            You rook'd my Godd — and you slew my Lovelass.
            Come here, Fengo, you Cancer o the Earth.

> *Commotion.*

            Nobody move! Drop your weapons!
            Forward Slaughterlord — I'll cutt you from this realm.

PAAVO   Hold, stand back — beware the rage of heathens.

FENGO   Never mind, I'll address the boy meself.

HORVENDAL   You got no right to be wearin that Cross.

FENGO   Boy, let us negotiate like civilized men.

HORVENDAL   Never, Fengo! Kneel! Get yer just dessertt!
            Brace yerself. It's gonna fuckin hurtt.

FENGO   Boy, I begs ye, have mercy on a old sinner.

HORVENDAL   Don't tell us. Tell it to Jesus Christ.

FENGO   Haill Lord Horvendal — thou art most fitt for Lord!
Haill Lord Horvendal — and so let fall thy Sword.

> *FENGO kneels. HORVENDAL raises the sword.*

PETRI   Peace, fiend of Denmark! Touch not that goodlie Man!
As Jesus spake of Mercie, you will not raise your hand!

FENGO   Nay, it seems that Martyrdom's my Fate.
Love, as ever always, must be devour'd by Hate.

HORVENDAL   Ohhhhh dear Uncle — at last is come the day.

PETRI   No! We'll not allow this! Stand infidel — AWAY!!

> *A Viking stabs HORVENDAL from behind.
> Other Vikings follow. HORVENDAL lashes
> violently at them all.*

HORVENDAL   Ug...

PAAVO   O savage, O monster, O beast!!

HORVENDAL   O villanie, O vileness, O horror!!

> *BROTHER PETRI seizes a wooden cross out of
> the ground. Impales THE MAD BOY from
> behind. The crowd gasps. HORVENDAL drops
> to his knees, skewered on the dragon-headed
> cross. Pause.*

PETRI   And so die all murderers.

VIKING   I int no murderer, Fengo, he swung at me first.

FENGO   Of course, man, of course.

PETRI   Shhhh! The heathen speaks.

                 Pause.

HORVENDAL   Ohhh Death...oh Shining-Hope escaped us...
                 This little storm-bark's finally run aground...
                 Hear me Denn-Mark! Behold my spatter'd Fate:
                 If Fengo stands for Mercy,
                 Then Madd Boy dies — for Hate.

                 He spits blood at FENGO.

                 Liljaa...

                 He dies. Pause.

FENGO   Well done, my Christian Soldiers.

PETRI   Hail Fengo!

ALL   HAIL!!

PAAVO   Oh wise and noble Lord,
                 How art we saved from barbarous destruction!

PETRI   Art well, Lord Fengo — art thou unscraped?

FENGO   Of course, Good Holy Brother, thou hast serv'd me
                 well.

PAAVO   Praise God!

VIKINGS   HAIL FENGO!!

VIKING   Fengo the Confessor — Saviour of the Danes!

ALL   HOORRAYY!!

Pause. FENGO stands forth. Drums sound.

FENGO   If aught of woe or wonder you've beheld,
Then look upon this tragic speckticall;
Let a stone be raised upon this barren ground,
Telling this, the sadd and sorry tale of our children:
These boys lie, and soon will be cremated,
Consum'd by Hatred, festring in their Hearts:
How many others walk about us in our midst,
With secret venom, welling in their souls?
Let these deaths stand as grim example to us all,
And their tale retold, till the termination of the world...
The guilty are all dead, the grieving are consoled:
May Jesus Christ Almighty have mercy on our
Souls.
Amen.

ALL   Amen.

*Music. The company proceeds out. The stage is
dark, empty, littered with the dead. The wind
howls. Blackout.*

The End.

***

Afterword

Review by Martin Morrow - *Calgary Herald*,
Monday, February 6, 1995.

A Viking free-for-all

There's method to the madness in this hilarious new play!

Imagine Hamlet, prince of Denmark, as a grungy teenage barbarian who pretends to be a dog. Think of his wicked uncle, King Claudius, as a slobbering, lecherous Viking lord who looks like Long John Silver crossed with a particularly obnoxious Hell's Angel. And fancy Polonius, the king's trusted counsellor, as a fawning old idiot whose sage advice to his son is, "Don't do anything stoopid, lad, it ain't wise."

Is this yet another misguided interpretation of Shakespeare? "Hamlet" for the "Dumb and Dumber" crowd?

No, it's "Mad Boy Chronicle", an audacious hilarious new play making its debut in a wild and often exhilarating production at Alberta Theatre Projects playRITES '95 festival.

Toronto playwright Michael O'Brien's rough, irreverent retelling of literature's most famous tragedy owes less to Shakespeare than to the Bard's ancient source: the tale of Amleth found in the "Gesta Danorum", a 13th Century Latin collection of Danish history and legend by Saxo Grammaticus. But this crazy Viking free-for-all is no more straight Saxo than it is straight Shakespeare. At times it resembles nothing so much as a Monty Python parody of a Norse legend, with ragged old crones who tell the dead king's ghost to "piss off" and a dumb-blond Viking warrior who talks to his sword.

But, to borrow a line from the Shakespeare "Hamlet", O'Brien's comic madness has method in it. Set in the Denmark of 999 AD, when Christianity was beginning to sweep through Europe, "Mad Boy Chronicle" grows from its initial spoof into something meatier: a reflection on how we twist and pervert religion to achieve our own ends. Lord Fengo, the Claudius figure here, doesn't just usurp the Danish throne, he also usurps the new belief and uses it to serve his own evil purposes.

Fengo, played here in a gigantic, juicy, over-the-top performance by Hardee T. Lineham, likewise seizes the story from its rightful hero, his nephew Horvendal (i.e. Hamlet), the "mad boy" out to avenge his father's murder.

Instead of suffering Hamlet's crisis of conscience, Horvendal is torn between his pagan thirst for revenge and the confusing new messages of peace and forgiveness contained in Christ's teachings. The guileful Fengo has no such problems. Sniffing out those aspects of Christianity which will be to his advantage, he happily embraces them and conveniently ignores or distorts the rest. In one side-splitting scene, he piously recites the words of wisdom from Ecclesiastes which, in his garbled version, come out as a sanction for everlasting violence.

Writing in a crude, obscenity-pocked prose, with occasional snatches of simple, sing-song verse, O'Brien amusingly debases the exquisite poetry of Shakespeare. Meanwhile, his plot keeps us entertained with its Viking variations on the familiar events and characters in "Hamlet". His heathen lunkheads are big on actions, not contemplation. Even the Ophelia character, Lilja, is given a gutsy, spirited personality. Here's a girl who'd rather lop off her father's head than quietly drown in a river.

Bob White's staging is raw, raucous and full-blooded, spilling forth bubbling comedy like an overturned hogshead of wine. Most of his brutish actors talk in mongrel accents that sound much less than Danish than a kind of bastard Irish, but it scarcely matters - authenticity clearly isn't the point here. They fill the stage with rude comic vitality, led by the towering Lineham who gnaws great hunks out of the scenery in his role as the gross but wily Fengo, whose way of charming the ladies is to show them the empty eye socket under his eyepatch.

While O'Brien's Vikings may be numbskulls, his principle characters are not mere cartoons, and the actors show us their dimensions.

Shaun Smyth's likeable Horvendal is both a troubled young man searching for belief, and a petulant teenage rebel, angry that his uncle has appropriated his radical new faith. As his mother Gerutha, Gale Garnett both sends up the maternal histrionics associated with Shakespeare's Gertrude and captures the helplessness of an ineffectual woman in a macho-male society. And a superb Les Carlson plucks unexpected chords of sympathy in his role as Fengo's toadying advisor and Lilja's abusive father, who shows latent twinges of feeling beneath his violence and stupidity.

Some will be offended by this play — most likely by a scene in which a vision of a thorny-crowned Jesus appears to Horvendal and tells him to forget what he's read in the gospels and kill his uncle. But for those who can tell the difference between wanton blasphemy and a pointed look at the abuse of Christianity, O'Brien's bold comedy is fresh, funny, fascinating and one of the best to come out of this nine-year-old festival.

***

This review by Martin Morrow won the 1995 Nathan Cohen Award for Theatre Criticism in the Short Review category, from the Canadian Theatre Critics Association.